10 RULES OF KARATE

THE IMMUTABLE PATH TO VICTORY

10 RULES OF KARATE

THE IMMUTABLE PATH TO VICTORY

Kris Wilder &
Lawrence A. Kane

Stickman Publications, Inc.
Seattle WA 98126

www.stickmanpublications.com
ISBN-13: 978-0-578-83362-0

Praise for 10 Rules of Karate...

"*10 Rules of Karate* is a book for readers who like it straight. The authors point out very clearly the why, what and how in karate when it comes to an unavoidable physical fight. Since losing isn't an option on or off the mat, this is an absolute must read for *karateka*." — **Christian Wedewardt**, Founder and Head of Karatepraxis (Frechen, Germany)

"In your hands is a book that cuts straight through the chatter and gets to the point of unarmed self-defense. No relying on luck, no need for hoping that strength alone will carry the day. This is advice, as straight as it gets, which gets to the heart of what is important, and despite the title is applicable regardless of martial arts style or system. Wilder and Kane have a down-to-earth, straight-forward approach that makes this book both readable and informative. You will have moments of, 'Why didn't I think of it like that before,' and other moments where you feel that the scales have been removed from your eyes and you can see clearly for the first time. For the beginner martial artist or the seasoned veteran this book holds much value. Read. Absorb. Keep what is useful. The rest will take care of itself." — **Wallace Smedley**, *hung gar kung fu* master instructor, *taekwondo* 3rd *dan*, Kickstart Kids instructor (Dallas/Fort Worth, United States)

"Understanding your 'why' or purpose for martial arts training is key. *10 Rules of Karate* serves as a vital self-defence roadmap in guiding you to an inevitable destination: to end violence immediately! Wilder and Kane, both prolific authors and active martial artists, have synthesized decades of their industry-proven experience to bring you 10 must-have principles to integrate into your martial arts and self-defence curriculum. Get the book. I did!" — **Chris Hanson**, Founder of Karate Unity (Toronto, Canada)

"The beauty of *dojo* training is also its biggest weakness outside the *dojo*. Wilder and Kane masterfully take the safe, structured lessons of karate and show how they must adapt to survive the chaos of real-world violence. Weaving together boxing principles, samurai wisdom, tactics of warfare and even marketing strategy, they establish a seamless and immutable path to victory. Highly recommended!" — **Goran Powell**, 5th *dan Goju Ryu* karate, Writer of the Year British Martial Arts Awards 2017 (London, England)

"A MAN CANNOT
UNDERSTAND THE
ART HE IS STUDYING
IF HE ONLY LOOKS
FOR THE END RESULT
WITHOUT TAKING THE
TIME TO DELVE DEEPLY
INTO THE REASONING
OF THE STUDY."

⊛ MIYAMOTO MUSASHI ⊛

TABLE OF CONTENTS

FOREWORD

by Rory Miller

Rory Miller is the author of several works on self-defense, including the seminal Meditations on Violence. He is a former Corrections sergeant and former contractor for the Iraqi Corrections Service under the Department of Justice's ICITAP program. Retired, he now lives peacefully in the Pacific Northwest.

THIS IS THE MOST FRUSTRATING BOOK KRIS Wilder and Lawrence Kane have ever produced. I got excited by the list of chapters. There's more violence wisdom in those ten chapter titles alone than you'll find in five average martial arts books. Then I dug in.

Let's just say that Messrs. Wilder, Kane and I are going to have a "spirited discussion" next time we get together.

"Presumptive Entanglement?" Hell, yah! Fights are messy and you get grabbed and slammed and pinned up against things and if you can't hit and control effectively in that goat screw, you're useless. And then the chapter pretty much ignores that stuff and talks about target fixation. What? Okay, entanglement is mental, too. And whereas physical entanglement requires two or more people (or one really, really clumsy one) you can mentally entangle yourself. And that makes you useless, too.

Only three possible reactions to a grab? Oh, my sweet summer child. There may only be three normal reactions to a stupid, unskilled, weak grab but if you know... But if you don't know, then, maybe it's better for you to be hitting than trying to unbalance or pin a threat on his heels, or extend a target so your strike does more damage.

So much good stuff in this little book. So much I disagreed with. Much of the disagreement comes from perspective: Infighters think differently than most modern karateka. Much of the disagreement comes from the writing. Like Miyamoto Musashi and Sun Tzu, the prose is often deliberately obscure, murky enough that you have to interpret it for yourself.

Oh, Wilder, Kane and I are going to have a discussion. And Kris is going to give me that smug grin of his and Lawrence is going to give that nasal micro-sigh and say, "You know, the discussion was really the point all along."

INTRODUCTION

"I can't sing and I can't dance, but I
can lick any SOB in the house."

Jack Dempsey (attributed)

The Fighter

WILLIAM HARRISON "JACK" DEMPSEY (1895 –
1983), nicknamed "The Manassa Mauler," was born into
an Irish family at Manassa Colorado in 1895. Boxing's
World Heavyweight Champion from 1914 to 1927, he
had 85 professional fights with a record of 68 wins (53 by
knockout), 6 Losses, and 11 draws. That's a 77.9% win-ratio
via knockout. If you were a professional fighter and went
toe-to-toe with Dempsey, there was close to an 80% chance
that you went to sleep. Further, if we counted correctly, 24
of Dempsey's opponents never even made it out of the first
round.

As Dempsey lit out on his own, leaving home at the age of
14, his fists quickly became his meal ticket. Odd jobs no
doubt helped meet his basic needs, but at the end of the
day his fists picked up the tab. Dempsey's achievements in
the squared circle were extraordinary. The bouts he fought
all across the Western United States and Canada as well
as amateur matches in various mining and logging camps
were legion.

This is how Dempsey earned his living as a young man, with his fighting skills. If he lost a match, not only did it hurt his body but it also left an ache in his belly as well. He quickly learned that the faster he won, the faster he earned the money he needed to get by. And, the less it hurt earning that money. It is hard to conceptualize this formula any simpler: win, and win fast.

Dempsey made his life in New York City after he retired from boxing. He opened a restaurant called Dempsey's. There he served as the nightly celebrity, glad-handing customers and signing autographs to attract clientele. It was a good life, one in which he assumed his fighting days were done. But, as fate would have it, they weren't quite over yet...

The story of Dempsey's mugging varies, as legends often do—about the number of muggers and exactly what he did—but in his autobiography Dempsey recounted that he was riding in a taxicab, heading home after a night at his restaurant when it happened. His driver stopped at a red light when two thugs rushed the vehicle from both sides, pulling open the cab's doors. Unfazed, Dempsey did exactly what he did best. He hit them with a flurry of punches, thwarting the intended robbery.

Today, with ubiquitous work and welfare, it's not all that hard to earn enough to eat. And most folks go a lifetime without facing any street violence. This dynamic has changed our martial arts... often not for the better.

The Irish Boxer and The Japanese Karateka

DEMPSEY WROTE A COUPLE OF BOOKS AND WAS the subject of several others. We recommend his

Championship Fighting, Explosive Punching, and Aggressive Defense, which was originally published in 1950 by Prentice Hall. Many years ago, Wilder showed Dempsey's *Championship Fighting* book to his karate *sensei* (instructor), a masterful practitioner who grew up and trained in post-war Japan.

After a few quiet moments perusing the boxing book, the Japanese man looked up and said, "This man knows karate." Clearly boxing is a western sport, not an eastern martial art, but many of the principles are the same, so much so that the son of an Irish immigrant from a small Colorado town and a Japanese martial artist who grew up in the firebombed ruins of Tokyo both saw fighting in much the same way. The underlying principles of striking and power generation were very much the same.

Dempsey had basic fighting skills that he learned from his father. He then sharpened those skills through battle. We use the term battle rather than competition because Dempsey started out by fighting hardened men in logging and mining camps and those rough and tumble altercations had hard edges that required immediate results. His winning philosophy can be seen in both his knockout ratio as a professional fighter as well as in how fast those knockouts were achieved in the ring. Dempsey and his boxing style were all about creating concussions, ending fights quickly.

To say that Wilder's *sensei* had tumultuous upbringing is a bit of an understatement. Like Dempsey, he learned his basic fighting skills from his father, but then went on to test what he'd learned on the streets, at times tangling with *yakuza* (members of organized crime syndicates). He also went "*dojo* busting," defeating other martial arts instructors in duels and then ransoming back their teaching certificates to earn a living. Although *kakidameshi* (dueling) was frowned upon, the practice was still tolerated in those days. Like Dempsey's boxing, his karate was all about creating concussions, about ending fights quickly.

Although one system operated with referees and rules, while the other did not, the underlying principles are very much the same. Both the Irish boxer and the Japanese *karateka* agree, principles win the day. You see, principles are precepts, they speak to the heart of any subject with all extraneous material swept away.

The Ten Precepts

THE TEN PRECEPTS IN THIS BOOK ARE ABOUT ending a physical confrontation as quickly as possible with empty-hand techniques. Our definition of "ending" is to make the attack stop. There is no running after the now fleeing assailant to catch him or her and strike them down. There is no lesson, no teaching, no therapy, no epiphany. There is only making that bad person or persons stop what they are doing instantly so that we will be safe. In other words, they are about ending fights quickly.

These precepts are a source of guidance to handling eventualities. For Dempsey, it was not situational being in a boxing ring or in the back of a cab. His principles drove his tactics. The tactics are specific pieces of information. If we could read Dempsey's mind, we likely would not understand the lower levels of his brain talking to itself, but it might sound something like this, "Attack, hit hard, keep hitting." That is principle.

There is often confusion in the martial arts world between principles and tactics. Instructors often give the difference between principles and tactics short shrift and as a result misunderstanding occurs. Without crucial clarity, stubborn adherence to what is perceived as a principle but is actually tactic can be adhered to. This may appear to work well in the safe confines of the *dojo* (training hall), but tends to end badly when pressure-tested.

Here's the deal: strategy is a plan of action, especially for obtaining a goal like winning a fight. It is derived from immutable principles, the underpinning elements that make everything else work. Tactics, on the other hand, are expedient means of achieving an end. They are low level and immediate. In other words, strategy is what we do to prepare for contact with an adversary while tactics are what we do during battle.

Practicing any martial arts from tactics upward to principles creates a house of cards that will collapse from a gentle breeze, whereas working downward from principles into tactics builds a strong foundation that can weather near any storm. When our principles have to work or we don't eat, clarity occurs. As a result, we fail and we starve, or worse... Or we survive and thrive, passing things down to our students. That is exactly what happened with the founders of classical styles like *Goju Ryu, Kenpo, Kyokushin, Shito Ryu, Shorin Ryu, Shotokan, Uechi Ryu,* and *Wado Ryu* to name a few.

This book is not large, yet the ideas within it are profound. They are based on time-honored, pressure tested principles that strengthen any fighting art from boxing to karate and more... They are not restricted solely to karate.

Integrating these precepts into one's martial style, however, may not be easy, even after due thought and consideration. The challenge is that experienced practitioners have years of training. This practice builds predilections, internalized patterns and behaviors, some of which may prove to be less than ideal when viewed through the lens of these precepts. It's easy to discard, to dismiss a principle that doesn't seem to fit, yet those who choose to work with the principles will find swiftness, clarity, and victory in so doing.

CHAPTER 1

WIN BEFORE YOU GO IN

"Victorious warriors win first and then
go to war, while defeated warriors go
to war first and then seek to win."

Sun Tzu

Go No Sen

IN JAPANESE, THE TERM, *GO NO SEN* MEANS blocking and riposting (receiving an attack and then striking back). It is a common method of martial arts practice, one that is great for training. At the beginning of a practitioner's martial arts adventure, *go no sen* looks simple. When the attacker initiates a blow, the defender stops the attack and then returns fire.

This dance has 3 stages: attack, block, and counter. The issue in real life is that unlike in the training hall the attacker doesn't stop. The initial assault is followed up by another attack and then another in rapid succession, oftentimes making for an overwhelming assault. This is not a tick-tock sort of affair, a give-and-take with each person taking their turn. The assailant uses initiative and surprise to gain momentum and successive attacks to prevail.

Fail to Follow-Up is Fatal

IN THE SPORTING WORLD NO BOXER WHEN given an opportunity will fail to follow up. A boxer will exploit every opportunity that their opponent presents. The boxer's goal is to end the event as fast as possible, to win at minimal cost. This is a great example of how sports can mirror confrontations in the real world.

You see, a criminal attacker has a similar agenda as does pretty much every thug or bully we might encounter. These folks are not interested in a fair fight; fighting is simply a means to an end. That means resources or resolution.

When they are trying to gain a resource, criminals prefer an assassination to a fight. That does not mean that they are always trying to murder their prey, but rather that they want to end the fight as quickly as possible without any risk to themselves. Ideally victims never get to fight back, so there's nothing fair about it. Similarly, people in an emotional frenzy who choose to fight also seek quick resolution, oftentimes a beatdown that makes them feel superior to those who have slighted them.

Be it in the ring, on the street, or pretty much anywhere else for that matter, fights continue until one or both of the parties involved surrenders, is injured to the point where he or she cannot continue to battle, is rendered unconscious, or killed. This means that failure to follow-up can be (and often is) fatal.

Basic Training

GO NO SEN IS GOOD AND IT IS USEFUL FOR BASIC training because it helps us learn movement and positioning.

Go no sen also stresses fundamentals, building what we in shorthand call muscle memory. It is not, however, much good in a fight.

When we look at higher-level martial artists performing *go no sen* it appears that they are receiving the attack before responding just like beginners. Without exception, however, they have actually combined a movement within their *go no sen,* turning it for all intents and purposes into *sen no sen* (which means intercepting the attack once it is on its way). Using this method, they move from reactive to responsive technique, placing themselves into a strategically superior position. This is the bare minimum we must achieve in real-world confrontations in order to prevail.

Three Elements

THE ILLUSTRATION BELOW SHOWS THE CLASSIC three elements of the *go no sen* pre-attack position. The strike, the block or arresting movement that stops the attack from landing, and then the counter strike. For example, an attacker may start with a head strike which is blocked and then countered with a chest punch.

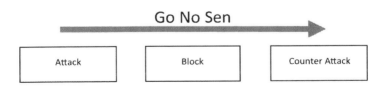

Figure 1: Go No Sen (Reactive Initiative)

The diagram below illustrates what should happen with a more advanced interpretation of the technique, however, one which leapfrogs momentum to turn a reactive movement into a responsive technique. The gray area shows what is unseen by the casual observer, the shadow adjustment that moves from *go no sen* (reactive initiative) to *sen no sen* (simultaneous initiative). This is where a change of position leapfrogs the attacker's initiative, assuring that the defender's counterattack has a good chance to succeed.

Using the previous head strike example, the defending practitioner might shift slightly offline and forward towards his or her adversary such that movement alone makes the head punch miss. Now what would have been an upward block can become a forearm strike to the head followed by the chest punch, so instead of blocking and riposting we move once and strike twice. This *sen no sen* interpretation is a massively more effective sequence for real-life self-defense than the back-and-forth that is demonstrated in the exact same drill with *go no sen*.

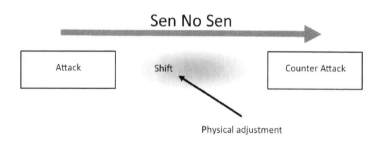

Figure 2: Sen No Sen (Simultaneous Initiative)

Knowing this, videorecord a tandem drill practice session or find a skilled practitioner demonstrating one on YouTube and then watch it in slow motion. Identify the shadow adjustment, the change in position and initiative that makes the application work. Later as you become more accustomed to observing this phenomenon, you can watch free sparring at speed and discover this same shadow adjustment.

When an experienced practitioner wants to counter a surprise attack, he or she will use this shadow adjustment to gain initiative. If you see no shadow adjustment, you are looking at an unrealistic drill, one which fails to honor the vital principle of winning before you go in. This honors Sun Tzu's admonition such that even when we are ambushed, we can successfully turn the tide on our attacker, winning before we go in.

TRAIN FOR VICTORY

IF WE MOVE UP THE CONTINUUM FROM *GO NO sen* (reactive initiative) to *sen no sen* (simultaneous initiative) we improve our chances of success in a fight, yet the ultimate aim of defensive technique is truly *sen-sen no sen* (preemptive initiative), which means cutting off an attack before it even starts.

Sen-sen no sen uses an adversary's "tell" (pre-assault change of energy) to sense that an attack is forthcoming and then cut it short before the threat has the chance to transform his or her mental desire to attack into the physical movement necessary to execute that desire. To the untrained observer, this looks a whole lot like a preemptive strike, yet to experienced practitioners the defensive nature of the application is clear. And, this is precisely what we must strive for in practice.

A common example of this pre-attack indicator many people experience is that someone who was glaring at us with direct eye contact suddenly looks away, or someone who was agitated suddenly becomes calm. Subtler examples may be an abrupt change in the person's breathing or the sudden development of a pallor or flushing of their face (paling is adrenaline-induced vasoconstriction, reddening is vasodilation). Within moments fists will fly.

It is perfectly acceptable and useful to teach *go no sen* to beginners, yet for experienced practitioners to practice with reactive initiative is folly. What we practice in the training hall is what we are most likely to do in real life. In order to win, we must train to win. Anything less is unacceptable. In tandem drills, sparring, and *kata* (solo practice) our focus must always be on controlling initiative in order to prevail in a fight.

CHAPTER 2

PRESUMPTIVE ENTANGLEMENT

"If you strike upon a thought that
baffles you, break off from that
entanglement, and try another, so shall
your wits be fresh to start again."

Aristophanes

Letting Go is Hard

JUDO TRAINING PRACTITIONERS OFTEN ENGAGE in *newaza* (groundwork). This groundwork is a subset of the system's *katame-waza* (grappling techniques), which includes *osae komi waza* (hold-down techniques) and *kansetsu waza* (joint locks). As the name implies, these techniques are all performed on the ground, used to hold an opponent down and disable his or her movement in order to win a match.

In the early beginnings of Kris's *newaza* training he found himself on top of his opponent, wrenching on his arm. His attempts to pry the other man's arm loose in order to get an armlock were not developing as he had hoped. While he futilely yet doggedly struggled with his plan of attack, one of the black belt instructors walked up and paused, gazing down at the situation. After a few moments he said, "You should let that go and move on to something else."

Sound advice, but unexpected in that moment. Kris had locked himself into an assumption of how he believed things were going to work, yet the idea in his head was not coming to fruition in reality. That's pretty normal, especially for inexperienced practitioners. We get an idea and over-focus on implementing it to the exclusion of other, better options. But, as the old saying goes, "If you find yourself in a hole, stop digging."

A Fancy Idea for Lying to Yourself

A MORE ACADEMIC WAY TO LOOK AT presumptive entanglement is through the lens of the sunken cost fallacy. In economics and business decision-making, a sunk cost refers to money that has already been spent and cannot be recovered. The sunken cost fallacy is the tendency for people to continue pursuing an idea or project even after it is clear that it cannot or will not succeed (meet its intended purpose) because we have already invested so much in that project. This fallacy can be seen in bridges, transportation projects, and other public works where the actual cost far, far exceeds the original estimate yet stakeholders merely shrug and say, "Well, we've already come this far..."

The judo coach pointed this fallacy out to Kris with his simple statement, "You should let that go and move on to something else." Unfortunately, many martial arts instructors fail to differentiate between logical and illogical training drills and methods because they do not take into account the challenge of presumptive entanglement.

Presumptive entanglement uses the same psychological blind spot as the sunken cost fallacy, but in a more hazardous way. You see, this flaw takes the adversary for granted, deliberately creating a false environment in which to flourish which makes us believe that our applications can stand the test of the real world when they cannot.

For instance, experienced *judoka* become exceptionally good at throwing their opponents in tournaments because they routinely practice against people who resist throws in training. That's good, laudable even, as long as we are only practicing for competition. The challenge is that one of the most common ways in real life to resist a throw is to punch an adversary in the face. *Judoka* don't regularly practice against that since punches are outlawed in the sport.

Every System has a Method

SPEAKING IN BROAD TERMS EVERY MARTIAL arts drill has a protective action built into it to allow for safer training. Think of it as a pressure release valve, a means of allowing action up to a certain point, and then the action is removed, stopped, or transformed to prevent injury. A sport can be played multiple times because it is designed to allow the participants to both train and participate in competition repeatedly over time.

Combat is not designed this way. Training for combat does have the pressure release valves, of course, but in actual combat those release valves are removed. In firearms training, for instance, we can wear special safety gear and use Simunition® for force-on-force training, then replace the non-lethal rounds with real bullets for use in the field.

In the earlier *newaza* example where his technique didn't work, Kris's opponent was restricted in his responses. He was not allowed to gouge Kris's eyes out, bite him, or grab his testicles. You can undoubtedly think of many other options, any of which would work but are illegal according to the rules of judo hence not attempted by his training partner. That safety valve made the drill valuable training for tournaments, but could easily lead to unrealistic assumptions should the *judoka* involved find themselves in a similar altercation on the street.

But what if we were to change things up a bit? Take the idea of presumptive entanglement but apply it to combatants who are standing and facing each other and we find a way to move past the sunken cost fallacy and directly address presumptive entanglement.

Presumptive Entanglement

WHEN WE UNDERSTAND AND IDENTIFY presumptive entanglement in our training, we are able to maintain the necessary safety valves in the *dojo*, but release them on the street when required to do so. We must be consciously aware of all the intentional flaws in our drills. Generally, they fall into one or more of the following three buckets:

1. Intentional pressure release in practice situations
2. Intentionally compliant participants
3. Intentionally overlooking the fragility of complexity

While judo often focuses on groundwork, karate uses many of the same type of entanglements standing up. For example, *kotegaishi* (wrist lock throw), a ubiquitous technique made famous by *aikido* that is also found in *jujitsu*, karate, and many other martial arts, might be used to demonstrate how a person can be thrown with the simple flick of a wrist. But, it's also a great example of where these three presumptive entanglement factors—pressure release, compliant participants, and fragile complexity—can be baked in.

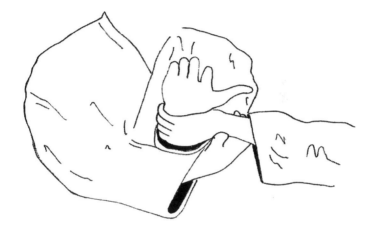

Figure 3: Kotegaishi (Wrist Lock Throw)

Pressure Release

Kotegaishi is a supinating wristlock which requires practitioners to grab a hold of their adversary's arm (typically but not always with both hands), bending and twisting to execute the technique. Executed properly it can break an opponent's wrist and dislocate their elbow and/or shoulder, but that means that pressure applied to the opponent's wrist must move up through their elbow and shoulder before transferring energy into their body. Consequently, we must use a compound movement, one which requires all three joints to work together, in order to make the throw possible.

Any angle or movement that is suboptimal allows for energy leakage which may thwart our technique… which is beneficial when we don't want to cause dislocation or joint damage, but not so much when causing that damage is our goal. Working with a compliant partner we may not realize that we are inadvertently undermining the throw via pressure release.

Compliant Participants

Oftentimes our training partner will throw him/herself to relieve the pressure, simultaneously avoiding injury while facilitating our technique. Or they might simply "tap out," ceding victory by acknowledging that our application would have been effective irrespective of whether or not it actually was.

Again, this is generally good for practicing safely, but can lead to a false confidence in the movement. If our technique will not work against a person who is actively resisting it will not hold up to real life application. There are ways to safely work around this in training, but the danger lies in not realizing when our training partner is being too cooperative.

Fragile Complexity

The more options an adversary has, the more fragile our technique becomes when truly put to the test. Let's face it, it's not possible to simply walk up to a resisting adversary, put him in a wristlock, and dump him onto the ground.

Consider all the ways he/she might fight back...

To begin, *kotegaishi* requires both of our hands to be brought to bear against one of our adversary's, which leaves their other hand unentangled. That free hand can be used to strike, slap, gouge, or otherwise thwart our technique. Or, our adversary they may simply move or shift in a way that relieves the pressure on their joints, countering our advantage. Or, the opponent might use his/her unencumbered knees, feet, or legs to strike us. Likewise, headbutts or bites may potentially be used as counters too. In real life, all these factors must be accounted for.

TRAIN FOR VICTORY

VIRTUALLY ALL ADDICTIVE BEHAVIORS, including gambling and substance abuse, share key neurobiological features which involve the neurotransmitter dopamine. Dopamine is tied to both reward and reinforcement, and can be affected by operant conditioning which is an associative learning process. Like the intermittent payoffs we achieve from gambling that can lead to addiction, *dojo* drills modify certain behaviors via reinforcement or punishment. It's good to build so-called "muscle memory" through patterns and repetition, but only to the extent that those patterns are useful for our intended application.

Martial artists use operant conditioning all the time, not only in drills but also in various *dojo* rituals that are found in traditional martial arts and to lessor degree modern combatives. There's nothing wrong with this so long as we take it in the proper context, understanding and questioning the presumptive entanglements that come with the territory. Never take these practices on blind faith. We must actively identify the intentional flaws in each and every drill and keep them firmly in mind when training.

When possible, we must practice with practitioners of other arts so that we will be able to handle a wide variety of styles and techniques rather than training to compete or battle against folks who fight just like us. In that same vein, we should practice against members of the opposite gender as well as people who are physically larger, smaller, older, and younger than we are from time to time too. More often than not if we're attacked on the street it will be by someone bigger, stronger, or more ferocious who believes that they can win, but threats come in all sizes and shapes so we must prepare for every eventuality.

CHAPTER 3

CRASH THE SYSTEM

"Inelegantly thrown acid is still thrown acid."

Mike Murphy

Ancient Samurai Wisdom

SOME OF THE GREATEST STRATEGIC WISDOM every provided about fighting comes from Miyamoto Musashi, Japan's most famous samurai, who wrote in Go Rin No Sho (The Book of Five Rings), "In battle, if you make your opponent flinch, you have already won." In other words, never let your opponent march at their chosen rhythm. Disrupt them. Crash the system...

Crashing the system has one goal, to stop the attacker from doing what he or she wants, making them flinch as Musashi wrote. Crashing the system causes disruption for the attacker by creating (1) multiple simultaneous setbacks, (2) creating one intense problem, or (3) creating many intense problems at the same time.

A System of Numerical Superiority

AN EXAMPLE OF CREATING MULTIPLE PROBLEMS comes from WWII. The German military built and deployed the most technologically advanced tanks the world had ever seen to support their war effort. Their Soviet adversaries adopted a different policy, however. They built lesser quality tanks, but more of them… a lot more. In fact, by mid-1941, the USSR had deployed more than 22,000 tanks—more tanks than found in all the armies of the world combined, and four times the number of tanks in the German arsenal.

Those Russian tanks were built so quickly, but with such low-quality tolerance, that in some instances a Soviet soldier could insert his finger between plates that formed its armored shell. A quote that is often attributed to Joseph Stalin is, "Quantity has its own quality." Their unsophisticated designs did have challenges with reliability, of course, but the strategy was to overwhelm the German tanks with superior numbers and it worked.

Crashing Your Own System

THE IMPACT OF ONE INTENSE PROBLEM CAN BE illustrated with the well-known and now classic episode in American business, home entertainment. Blockbuster dominated the home movie and video game rental market for two decades, but failed to innovate. When Netflix and Redbox first appeared, they competed more-or-less on parity, but made inroads since they charged no late fees (which at one point accounted for 16% of Blockbuster's revenue). Then, along came streaming services and new competition and that broke the equation for good.

It is interesting to note that Blockbuster considered buying Netflix for $50 million at one point, but ultimately blew that opportunity in deciding that the purchase price was too steep. Between 2003 and 2005 they lost 75% of their market value, ultimately declaring bankruptcy by 2010. Today, all of their stores but one have been closed, with that remaining location turned into an Airbnb. Like Blockbuster, we often pass over the opportunity to avoid crashing our own system but only recognize it with hindsight.

Many Problems

THE CREATION OF MANY INTENSE PROBLEMS AT one time can be illustrated with Operation Desert Storm. On November 29, 1990, the United Nations Security Council authorized the use of "all necessary means" of force against the nation of Iraq if it did not withdraw from Kuwait which they had illegally invaded. When Iraqi President Saddam Hussein defied that order, the world responded with a massive US-led air and land offensive, Operation Desert Storm.

Even though Iraq began the war with the world's 5th largest standing army, their military might was gutted in a bit less than four days, with ultimate collapse coming a month-and-a-half later. You see on January 17, 1991 the US, its NATO allies, and a coalition of Arab countries, some 35 nations in all, used stealth bombers, cruise missiles, laser-guided "smart" bombs, and other sophisticated technology to overwhelm the Iraqi forces. By the time a cease-fire was declared 42 days later, the Iraqi forces had all either surrendered or fled.

Reading the Opponent's Textbook

WHEN HE WAS WORLD HEAVYWEIGHT Champion, "Iron" Mike Tyson was definitively the best boxer in the world. Tyson could hit hard, but so could other greats like Ernie Shaver, Evander Holyfield, George Foreman, Hasim Rahman, Ingemar Johansson, Lennox Lewis, Manny Pacquiao, Muhammad Ali, and Tyson Fury. Every boxer has their individual style and we can see a record of it. Nearly everything about boxing is recorded in some way, statistics like each fighter's height, weight, reach, handedness, win/loss records, knockouts, decisions, proclivities (e.g., affinity for throwing jabs, uppercuts, etc.), and the like is dutifully recorded.

Whether the boxer is orthodox or unorthodox, what they prefer to do in any given situation, whether they are they closers, or jabbers, even their stamina, it is measured. All of this information is recorded in a book of statistics. Consequently, when preparing for a boxing match every boxer and his/her coaches have plethora of information to rely on, insight into their forthcoming opponent that can help them up their game.

In self-defense situations, however, no such textbook exists. We cannot pre-scout our adversary and ascertain his or her tendencies. We cannot know for certain how many assailants there will be, when or where they will attack, or by what means and methods they will strike. However, broad assumptions can be made and we are able to act upon a combination of our assumptions and observations to be as prepared as possible.

Disrupt and Deny

REGARDLESS OF THE PREDICAMENT WE FIND ourselves in, our ultimate strategy must be to deny the other person or persons whatever they want to do, while doing what we want to do, during the fight. Whether it's boxing, other combative sports, or simply a game of pickup basketball, the principle remains the same. Never let your opponent march to his or her chosen rhythm.

Denying an adversary what they want to do is where crashing the system comes in. Crashing the system is a way of disrupting the other person's plan. Crashing the system is about making the adversary have to stop what they want to do and respond to whatever it is we're throwing at them. Crashing the system takes our opponent out of his or her game. It knocks the threat back on his or her heels so that they have to respond, reset, or readjust. In other words, it makes the assailant do what they don't want to do.

The Straight Blast

CRASHING THE SYSTEM INVOLVES NO DANCING around. There is no grab the wrist, spin it this way, turn here, pivot there, tap the back of the knee, and then do the hokey-pokey to make the other guy fall down. Crashing the system is flat out aggression designed to deny your opponent whatever they want to do.

A great example of this was Bruce Lee's straight blast (straight punch). His style, while very much his own, was rooted in *wing chun,* a Chinese *kung-fu* system that emphasized fast hands and attacking the adversary's centerline. Striking the centerline as fast and as hard as he could, Lee was able to disrupt and disable his opponents.

Grip-and-Go

JUDO IS ONE OF THE FEW SPORTS THAT CAN BE easier to perform blindfolded than sighted as practitioners are trained to sense their opponent's micromovements, shifts in balance, direction, or center of gravity, when determining the best course of action to disrupt their designs and win the match. Sensitivity to tiny postural changes is key. Our judo *sensei,* Kenji Yamada, used to say crash the system in a different way because his context was sport rather than combative. His admonishment was, "Grip-and-go."

Grip-and-go meant that we were supposed to grip our opponent's *gi* (uniform) and before they could sense our initiative we would immediately launch into our technique. This immediate action would oftentimes preclude an opponent's ability to counter. Straight blast, grip and go, they're both examples of crashing the system in a martial arts context.

It's Not Pretty

CRASHING THE SYSTEM IS NOT ABOUT ELEGANCE. As the quote says at the beginning of this chapter states, "Inelegantly thrown acid is still thrown acid." It's about function, whether it succeeds more-or-less as planned or flat out doesn't work. Crashing the system is not about the perfect move, the elegant, picture-perfect act, it is about getting something on the adversary to change the moment. To enable us to prevail…

Win pretty or win ugly and it's still a win. But if we allow the pursuit of perfection to keep us from acting decisively, we are almost certain to lose.

Everyone tends to develop a "go to" technique, something they're comfortable with using under pressure. It could be a straight blast, grip-and-go, or something completely different such as an elbow strike, finger whip, eye gouge, or as the illustration above shows, an uppercut. Clearly punching a hard chin in this fashion is going to hurt, possibly even break a bone or two in your hand, but if it knocks the other guy out, we'll call it a win.

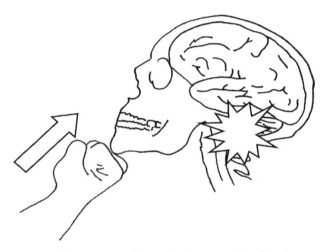

Figure 4: Crashing the System (Knockout)

Crashing the system is about working big to small, finding a way to stop the attacker from doing what he or she wants to do and then making every effort to exploit that moment and in doing so achieve victory. We cannot worry about pretty. We must not concern ourselves with perfection, save for in the sheltered confines of the training hall. Train for perfection but in practical application strive for effectiveness. On the street, that's all that matters.

TRAIN FOR VICTORY

EVERY PERSON HAS A BUILT-IN SYSTEM, AN attack system and a defense system. These methods are often untrained, buried in our brain's fight, flight, or freeze response. Some are more effective than others, and some can even be outright dysfunctional, but everyone has an instinctive system. With training as martial artists, our systems become quite a bit more sophisticated than ordinary citizens. We spend hours training defensive and offensive movements, leveraging the strategy and tactics of our martial styles.

While martial styles contain a wide variety of applications, unarmed fighting systems tend to fall into two big buckets, striking-centric systems (e.g., boxing, karate) and grappling-centric systems (e.g., wresting, jujitsu). Irrespective of tactics, the focus on these two divisions of hand-to-hand fighting systems is to create problems for any threats that practitioners face. This is why trained practitioners tend to perform better than untrained individuals in in real-life fights. But, fighting skills alone may not be enough.

When choosing a martial system for self-defense, it must be fit for purpose. While an art designed for sporting application likely can be utilized for self-defense, more often than not it will fall short of optimal. In other words, we must be able to remove any baked in pressure release, compliant participants, or fragile complexity (as we discussed in Chapter 2) such that we can physically stop a threat. And then, we need to crash the system to make it happen.

Further, if what we study does not cover the full range of pre- and post-event management, things like awareness, avoidance, de-escalation, creating witnesses, dealing with law enforcement, and navigating the legal system in addition to fighting, we will find ourselves underprepared. By training holistically and realistically we are best able to crash the other guy's system rather than our own and ultimately prevail.

CHAPTER 4

PIN TO WIN

"People should know when they're conquered."

Quintus (from the opening scene of the
Oscar-award-winning movie *Gladiator*)

Penalties for Breaking the Rules

PINS CAN BE VERY POWERFUL IN REAL-LIFE SELF-defense situations, but if we think like a wrestler or a judo player who has immobilized an opponent with a winning pin, we are visualizing sports. This may win tournaments, but it is not the correct version of pinning to apply in an actual fight. Pinning in a combative situation is the precursor to a final, fight-ending blow.

In sports, such as basketball, a player can get pinned into the corner of the court. They may not be able to successfully dribble their way out or pass the ball to another player. This pinning in the corner of the court is a successful pin for the team on defense. To stand in front of an oncoming player's position, however, will get the defender called for a blocking foul.

Similarly, in American football, a defender who blocks a receiver while not looking back at a thrown ball is going to earn a penalty. Even blocking the receiver's vision without touching him results in a penalty. In essence, the defender is playing the receiver and not the ball, which is considered unfair competition.

These types of penalties in sports can result in a significant loss (or gain depending on which side you're on) of field position. They can even affect the outcome of the competition. Both of these fouls are pins, obstructions to free movement that impede the flow of the game. Sometimes, however, what appears very much like a penalty is not assessed.

How many times have we heard a sports analyst or announcer point to a moment and say, "They just got tangled up?" In sports it is important for penalty assessment to know whether or not an act was intentional and to understand who was responsible for breaking the rules. In real life altercations there are rules too, but they're not the same. And, enforcement usually involves the judicial system not a referee.

Stickiness verses Entanglement

ENTANGLEMENT IS NOT PINNING AND PINNING is not entanglement. Miyamoto Musashi's famous *Go Rin No Sho* was split into five sections. In his second section, *The Book of Water,* he wrote, "When the enemy attacks and you also attack with the long sword, you should go in with a sticky feeling and fix your long sword against the enemy's as you receive his cut. The spirit of stickiness is not hitting very strongly, but hitting so that the long swords do not separate easily. It is best to approach as calmly as possible when hitting the enemy's long sword with stickiness. The difference between Stickiness and Entanglement is that stickiness is firm and entanglement is weak. You must appreciate this."

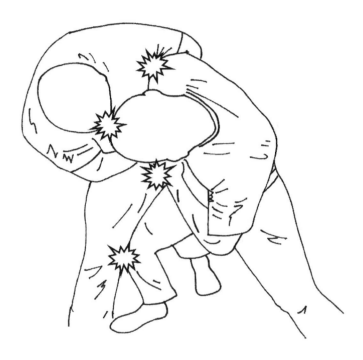

Figure 5: "Pinning" With Stickiness Not Entanglement

Indeed, as Musashi wrote, we must appreciate this. Stickiness, or pinning, is a strategic play, whereas entanglement is not only weaker but often unintentional. Let's delve a little deeper into how pinning actions can play out in real life...

In War and Peace

A SIEGE IS THE MILITARY TACTIC OF BLOCKADING a city or a town with an army over a prolonged period of time. In modern military terms this pinning action is the antecedent to surrender, but throughout most of human history it has portended massacre. In the Roman world, for example, a siege often ended in slaughter as examples needed to be made. Few were ever spared for resisting the will of the Roman empire; at times when angered sufficiently they would go so far as to leave no stone atop another, salt the fields, and only leave enough survivors to strike fear into the hearts of their enemies by relating the deed. The siege, the pin, that was the beginning of the end.

In civilian context police officers and security personnel routinely use pins to win too. A threat (bad guy) will be pinned against a car, a wall, or the ground, depending on whatever's convenient. This pin, however, is only a transitional situation. You see, the pin is a precursor to the final action. In this case it facilitates handcuffing, which is quickly followed by transition into the back of a police cruiser so that the suspect can be booked into jail and (more often than not) prosecuted.

In the Animal Kingdom

IN THE ANIMAL KINGDOM THE PIN IS ALSO A precursor to the final act. With big cats like lions, tigers, and jaguars, the pinning movement is used to achieve strangulation. When looking at pack animals such as hyenas, wolves, or coyotes, the group will work together to cut a prey animal from the protection of its herd, surround it, and then murder and eat their selected victim. The result is somewhat less elegant than with the big cats, but the method serves the same purpose. Once the victim is pinned, it's served for dinner.

TRAIN FOR VICTORY

A PIN IS A FANTASTIC FIGHT-ENDER, ONE THAT can be used in a variety of situations to place an adversary into a position where we may finish him or her off. With ubiquitous video surveillance and cellphone cameras, however, it can be risky legally as we can expect to be challenged on why we continued to fight after the threat appeared to be subdued.

There are two strategies for handling this contingency. The first is fight with our mouths too, using words that make it clear we are not the aggressor such as saying, "Stop attacking me." The second is to assure that the pin is momentary and transitional, not stopping the action in between the pin and the finishing move. In this fashion we both prevail in the fight and set ourselves up for a better chance of success in the aftermath.

Obviously, this strategy must be practiced for it to be effective on the street. How many times do we attempt to create witnesses while training techniques in the *dojo?* If the answer isn't often, that's an action to pursue immediately.

CHAPTER 5

JABS OVER GRABS

"A man strikes you, make him bleed. He
makes you bleed; you break his bones. He
breaks your bones, kill him. Being hit is
inevitable, strike back twice as hard."

Bruce Lee

All About Control

WHILE MOST KARATE SYSTEMS INCLUDE
grappling and groundwork, the art is primarily about
percussive violence and escape. That's why when we
analyze *kata* and application, we discover that roughly
70 to 90 percent of our techniques are applied with
strikes from our hands and feet. The remaining throws,
groundwork, pressure points, and the like round out the
system holistically, but are not our primary focus. Here's
why: Grabs quickly lead to entanglement, especially if
there is no strategic purpose behind them.

You see, grabbing is about control which can be useful in
many situations, but all too often it is incompatible with the
strategy of karate. That's bad, but in practical application it
gets worse when it comes to a street fight. You see, only one
of three possible outcomes of a grab betters our position.

Only One in Three

In gross terms, grabs generate three potential outcomes:

1. A grab can produce a responsive grab
2. A grab can initiate responsive flight
3. A grab can generate a responsive strike

Only one of these three outcomes, flight, improves our position during a violent confrontation. That means that in most circumstances we are far better off striking an adversary, save for times when we are using a grab to set up a strike or using the grab for a specific tactical purpose such as to restrain a suspect and hold him or her until the police arrive.

The location and intensity of a grab can indicate its purpose, exposing our intent and altering the other person's response to what we are attempting to do. For example, grabbing an extremity helps us control another person. Controlling their head is even better, but more hazardous to the subject, hence often deemed unallowable by authorities such as law enforcement officers in low-level force situations.

Consequently, wrist and armlocks, often performed in conjunction with verbal commands, are commonly used to restrain a threat. Because the subject of these techniques knows that there is authority behind the law enforcement or security officer using force on them, they are likely to comply.

In civilian context, however, we rarely have the authority to order a person to comply like a sworn officer is able to do, so an identical attempt to grab a limb may be met with fiercer resistance. That means that whenever we grab an adversary, we are using suboptimal technique, an application that does not leverage the strength of our karate training. A preference for jabs over grabs helps us resolve most confrontations in our favor.

Figure 6: Grabs Rarely Improve Our Position

We will delve a little deeper into these three potential outcomes, grab, flight, and strike, to expose their dynamics and a bit of the underpinning fight psychology involved...

A Person Who Grabs Back Wants to Fight

IF WE GRAB A PERSON AND THEY IN TURN GRAB us back, we are now in a fight or at least a fairly serious confrontation. This return grab can easily disrupt our plans. For example, it can drive the fight to the ground, which is not the strong suit of our karate fighting system. Consequently, we are not interested in going to the ground and should be cautious of entanglements with those who prefer that outcome. After all, as mentioned previously, our best chance to prevail is playing our game while keeping the adversary from successfully implementing his or her own.

Our goal should be staying upright, while knocking the adversary to the ground, preferably in an unconscious state. Our strategy of remaining standing is addressed in more depth in Chapter 6, but the key takeaway for the moment is that we must keep our feet during the fight, so grabbing a grabber is dysfunctional on multiple levels.

For those predisposed toward violence, our grab will almost certainly set them off. From there, our situation descends into chaos, which is by no means our friend whether we wind up on the ground or not. And, win or lose, we may face legal and/or civil consequences if our grab sparks violence. So, grabbing a grabber is a bad thing.

A Person Who Pulls Away Wants to Flee

WHILE A GRAB MAY ILLICIT ANOTHER GRAB, IT can just as easily generate a flight response where the person we grabbed pulls away. This flight response is based around a visceral understanding that the situation is not going to play out their way. Deep in that other person's psyche is the belief that our goal is inevitable, that if we get a hold of them, we will prevail. Consequently, their only option is to run away.

This instinctive response is common with small children. How many times have we seen a boy or girl pulling back from their parent's hold on their arm in a mall or shopping center? The same thing applies with grown adults who believe themselves outmatched, such as the junkie pulling away from a law enforcement officer even when they viscerally know that they have no chance of escape. Generally speaking, if a threat pulls away and attempts to flee, we are best off letting them go.

A Grab That Begets a Strike is "Game On"

WHEN A PERSON IS GRABBED AND THEY reflexively strike back, they likely come from a world where violence is a tool. They are comfortable with the proximity and the intimacy of hand-to-hand combat. The rules of in this world are simple, when offense is perceived instantly attack and do so with excessive proportion. Get violent, do it fast, and make it personal. Does this sound like someone we really want to tangle with? Likely not. But if we've grabbed someone who's instinctive response is striking back, we will have little choice but to go toe-to-toe with them.

A person whose instinctive fight, flight, or freeze response is to attack can be dangerous even if they have no martial arts or combative training or experience. You see, when people are faced with a perceived threat, their brain believes that they are in danger and their body automatically reacts with a response designed to keep them safe. This response may or may not be suited to the situation at hand, such as running from an aggressive, growling dog which may trigger an attack, but the hormone reactions produced by the autonomic nervous system in these cases make us stronger and more resilient in the face of whatever follows. Consequently, an untrained individual who mercilessly attacks back may easily injure or even kill a trained practitioner who is unprepared for the ferociousness of their response.

TRAIN FOR VICTORY

ALWAYS STAY TRUE TO THE STRATEGY OF YOUR art. For example, in Okinawan *Goju Ryu* karate which both authors practice, the fundamental strategy is to close distance, imbalance, and use physiological damage to incapacitate an adversary. While that may leave room for certain types of grabs for techniques such as momentarily posting an adversary's weight on one leg in order to blow out their knee with a joint kick, those applications are few and far between.

Roughly 70 percent of our art involves various hand techniques such as punches, elbow strikes, and forearm smashes, with 20 percent dedicated to kicks, knee, and leg strikes. That's about 90 percent percussive techniques, which means that our training should be 90 percent focused on using our hands and feet to prevail in a fight. We train enough in grappling, throwing, and choking to be competent, but that shouldn't be the primary focus of our practice... or yours.

Research the underpinning strategy of your art and keep it in mind while you train. Since all the art's tactics are built around this strategy, failure to follow it will almost certainly lead to failure in application. That means that everything from stances to movement to breathing, methods of power generation, and techniques such as punches, kicks, throws, and groundwork all rely upon a coherent, strategic framework and approach. Know it, use it, and improve your chances to prevail.

CHAPTER 6

HIM DOWN NOW

---

*"The reason lightning doesn't strike
twice in the same place is that the same
place isn't there the second time."*

Willie Tyler

Simple and Direct

"HIM DOWN NOW" IS A SIMPLE STATEMENT. THE phrase has no conjunctions, no ands, no buts, no equivocations, and no tangents. The phrase contains three words and is as clear and concise as it can possibly be.

Remove one word from it and it doesn't have the same meaning. In fact, the three-word phase ether loses its emphasis or its object. For example, remove the word "him" and the declarative two-word sentence loses its direction. It is a game we can play as we remove a word or two and see the loss of object or context, but our point here is to internalize the phrase not decipher it.

Animal Says

IT IS ALSO IMPORTANT TO BE CLEAR THAT THE phrase, "him down now" was laid on us by Marc MacYoung. If you don't know who he is, some background is in order. You see, growing up on gang-infested streets not only gave Marc his street name "Animal," but also extensive firsthand experience about what does and does not work in real life when it comes to self-defense. In fact, he was first shot at when he was 15 years old and has since survived multiple attempts on his life, including professional contract hits.

Over the years, Marc has held a number of dangerous occupations including working as the director of a correctional institute, bodyguard, and bouncer. A lifelong martial artist, he teaches experience-based self-defense to police, military, civilians, and martial artists around

Figure 7: Him Down Now

the world. His is also a prolific writer who codified the five stages of violent crime, is one of the world's foremost authorities on violence in society, and currently works as a court-recognized expert witness.

So, when a guy like that talks, we listen. And what he had to say has become foundational to how we practice and teach martial arts. It's not about techniques, but rather about strategy. That simple phrase makes it clear that in order to end a fight with minimal risk to ourselves or those we may be protecting we have to act quickly, aggressively, and with purpose. And, putting the other guy (or gal) on the ground is an excellent way of doing that.

Our Purpose

MARTIAL ARTS IN GENERAL, AND KARATE IN particular, can have many purposes. The question becomes, what are those purposes and how do we discern the difference between form and function? Beautiful form has little utility unless it functions as intended under pressure.

Karate can be practiced slowly and precisely, becoming very much like *tai chi,* just as *tai chi* can be performed swiftly and with great violence like karate, yet either one can be effective on the street. And, either one can be pursued for health and meditation benefits in addition to, or instead of, self-defense. Consequently, when training, our purpose and direction must be clear so that we are focused on the appropriate outcomes. If we wish to train for self-defense, that purpose must trump, but not necessarily replace, all the other aspects of our art.

Architecture Defines Purpose

ARCHITECTURE IS A GREAT, REAL-WORLD example of purpose in execution. For instance, the Bronze and Iron ages combined spanned roughly 1,100 years from about 1700 BC to 600 BC. The architecture of those times was dominated by the roundhouse (the dwelling, not the technique). Virtually everyone from peasants to princes utilized them.

The roundhouse was a fairly simple structure. Vertical posts were driven into the ground in a circle and then waddle and dob was applied. The waddle was a weaving of slender limbs that went in between the posts. The dob was made of mud, straw, hair, and dung which was blended together and then applied onto the inside and outside of the walls, in the same fashion as modern stucco, to create a smooth surface that protected inhabitants from the elements. The roof was applied in the shape of a cone, with a bit of overhang so that water would drip away from the walls during rainy season and not damage the roundhouse or its foundation.

A roundhouse was by no means elegant, but it was used for so long because it was simple and effective. It could be built by pretty much anyone with readily available resources, and required little in the way of tools or machining to put together. In contrast cathedrals were not living quarters like roundhouses, they were designed as holy places meant to inspire the populace.

The earliest medieval cathedrals were built in the Norman or Romanesque style, with heavy columns supporting great rounded arches, whereas Victorian cathedrals built later on are famous for their spires and intricate artwork. This style helped separate them from buildings designed for the people's day-to-day existence. Their architecture pulls visitors away from the mundane world and transports them to the sacred with soaring stone ceilings, archways, stained glass windows, and magnificent decorations.

Contrast between these two structures is both significant and profound. Karate needs to be the same, designed with clarity of purpose. All of the traditional Okinawan and Japanese karate systems were designed, built, and organized by their founders for one primary purpose, to end fights instantly. To put the other person on the ground and do it now.

Sure, there are other benefits that come with martial arts training, but we cannot self-actualize our way out of danger. Ending fights is the lens through which we must focus our training and judge the viability of our applications. Anything that does not immediately accomplish that objective has been misunderstood, misinterpreted, or misapplied.

Solve the Problem Quickly and Unequivocally

WHEN WE LOOK AT EFFECTIVE KARATE, THE main take away is that it needs to solve this one simple problem as efficiently as possible. Every movement during a violent altercation must further our goal of putting the adversary on the ground, preferably by knockout, so that we will remain safe. It's all about applying damage to another person's body that allows us to escape the danger that they represent.

Done properly, the adversary never gets a choice, never gets a turn, never has a chance. We impose our will, placing the threat in a reactionary position where he or she is unable to execute their intentions successfully. In doing so we implement Animal's declaration. It's all about him down now.

TRAIN FOR VICTORY

A CHALLENGE WITH TANDEM DRILLS IS THAT they must be realistic enough to reinforce proper application and street-worthy technique, yet safe enough that we do not injure ourselves or our training partners. Some practitioners like to use protective gear for this purpose, but even then, certain techniques like neck cranks must be curtailed in the name of safety. Consequently, we prefer a "one-step" drill where everything is on the table.

This drill is performed as a tandem exercise done in slow motion. One partner initiates a move and the other partner matches his or her speed making a single motion to respond. We each get only one movement before it becomes the other person's turn. React to the opponent's blows so that the ebb and flow of the fight is more-or-less realistic. The drill continues without resetting until the allotted time expires, or one person or the other end ups in a position from which they cannot continue and have to reset. Since our mindset is "him down now" that will presumably be a short period of time.

Even though we move slowly, it is vital to use proper body mechanics and targeting as well as to move at equal speed. It is okay to speed things up a bit, especially when working with experienced practitioners, so long as both partners are operating at the same speed, in control, and safe. Nevertheless, we should keep things slow enough that we have time to evaluate and take advantage of the "best" opening available and talk to each other so that we will learn what we are doing correctly in addition to discovering opportunities we may have missed during the exercise.

In this fashion we train to habituate good techniques. We can do the exact same things on the street, only faster and more forcefully. This drill should not become our only means of training, yet it is valuable enough to merit emphasis.

CHAPTER 7

THROWS THRASH, TAKEDOWNS COMPOUND

"In *randori* (free sparring) we learn to employ
the principle of maximum efficiency even
when we could easily overpower an opponent."

Jigoro Kano

Throws Versus Takedowns

THE IDEA THAT THROWS THRASH AND takedowns compound is based around the difference between the two techniques. A throw, by definition, means casting something away from yourself, especially to project or propel from one's hand using a sudden forward motion or straightening of the arm and wrist. That means that something you once held has suddenly left your grip but you are likely to remain at or near the spot from which you initiated the throw. Therefore, when we throw an opponent down onto the ground, we remain standing and in doing so gain a significant advantage.

A takedown, on the other hand, is a martial arts application that involves both combatants progressing from a standing position down onto the ground. One combatant may well be in control, say landing on top of the other, but at the end of the movement both people are on the ground. Using the example of hurling a ball, a takedown would involve throwing the ball to the ground at your feet without letting go. Slamming yourself into the ground while holding a ball in your hand makes for a ridiculous picture and simultaneously an undesirable tactic for *karateka*.

A Small Degree of Control

A THROW MAINTAINS VERY LITTLE IF ANY control of the adversary when he or she hits the ground. Imagine the classic judo throw *ippon-seoi-nage* (one-arm shoulder throw). Often the first throw taught to beginners, *ippon-seoi-nage* involves pulling one of your opponent's arms to unbalance him or her, turning into the opponent in an attempt to load him/her onto your back, carrying him/her up over your back, and then slamming him/her down onto the ground. This is all done while you remain standing. Often you will keep your grip on the opponent's arm you initially grasped in order to facilitate a finishing move, but you can just as easily let go.

Because judo is a sport and only a clean throw wins a full point, a follow-up technique such as a pin is almost always attempted. For more advanced practitioners these two moves, the throw and the pin, can be done near seamlessly. This makes the throw and the pin appear to be one smooth movement. This appearance can be deceiving for those who observe it, as the two distinct actions may appear as one. During the throw the *judoka* has very little control over his or her opponent, hence must move to the ground to achieve it and win the match.

Most karate systems utilize *ippon-seoi-nage* too, albeit slightly more violently than our judo counterparts. In practice we might keep ahold of our partner's arm to guide and soften their landing, but in combative application we almost always let go of our adversary after the throw, hoping that ground will knock the fight out of him or her while simultaneously assuring that we cannot be pulled down onto the ground with them. Depending on the unique circumstances we face we may additionally choose to close in and finish off the threat once they've hit the ground. The key point is that we have little control and slight contact with the adversary when executing this move, and only where and when we intend it.

Figure 8: Ippon-Seoi-Nage (One-Arm Shoulder Throw)

The High Ground of The Low Wrestler

UNLIKE A THROW, A TAKEDOWN HAS A VERY large degree of both contact and control. A good illustration of this is with a wrestler's classic, double-leg takedown. The double-leg takedown involves deeply penetrating the opponent's defenses, making hard contact with our shoulder, grabbing behind both of the opponent's legs, and driving him or her backward onto the mat. Done properly this technique not only knocks our opponent backward, pulling his or her feet out from underneath, but also lands us on top in a position of control once the movement is complete.

A critical difference between takedowns and throws is use of the high ground. Throughout history, controlling the high ground has been key to warfare. That is why castles and other fortifications were built on high ground with clean lines of sight to any threatening incursions. It is both easier and more accurate to shoot an arrow or throw a spear downward than upward. And, boiling oil is only effective when poured downward onto adversaries.

As with siege fortifications, holding the high ground in a one-on-one fight increases our choices whereas being on the low ground limits our options. Standing over an opponent is much better than looking up at them. Consequently, while takedowns can be effective, they do not guarantee that we will land in a superior position when we hit the ground. Throws are strategically better in general, and for karate practitioners in particular more so, as we tend to be much better at upright fighting than rolling around on the ground.

Going to the ground is dangerous in a fight, particularly when there is more than one adversary, hazardous terrain (e.g., rocks, broken glass, passing vehicles, discarded needles), or weapons involved. Consider the ancient battlefield. When a warrior lost his footing in battle, he often lost control of his primary weapon as well. That meant facing a highly-trained, armed, and armored opponent empty-handed from a position of severe disadvantage. To counter this, jujitsu evolved among the warrior class in feudal Japan specifically to deal with this challenge.

A Bad Situation Resolved Two Ways

LET'S SAY YOU WERE A SAMURAI AND FOUND yourself disarmed during a battle. If you could not retrieve your own sword, a top priority would be obtaining another one, often taking it from an attacker. One way of doing that was to use a throw. You would close distance, getting inside the sweep of the other guy's sword and in doing so positioning yourself for a hip or shoulder throw. A skilled adversary would try to block your technique or break his fall so as to not lose all advantage, of course, but if he failed and landed improperly the ground itself would cause damage. Either way you would be in an advantageous position to use your attacker's weapon against him or, failing that, break off your attack and try a different approach. Chances are at least decent that you would prevail.

A second option would be to go for a double leg takedown. As you close distance you risk both a killing blow from his sword as well as a disabling strike from its pommel. Assuming you make it through and are successful, you both tumble onto the ground. Even if you land in a dominant position, you risk assassination by one of his fellow soldiers as you struggle to gain control of his weapon because you cannot easily move or disengage. In fact, you will find yourself on near even odds grappling with a skilled adversary which means that even if you prevail you are likely to be injured in the process. With less options, your chances of survival are reduced.

As you can see, throws establish instant dominance whereas takedowns complicate the moment. Takedowns are for sports whereas throws are combative.

In other words, throws thrash while takedowns compound. Compounding an event adds complexity, making the quick win we seek far more challenging. The bottom line: if we're in a fight and the situation calls for dumping the other guy onto the ground, we must use a throw not a takedown.

TRAIN FOR VICTORY

IT'S EXTREMELY CHALLENGING TO GET A THROW in tournament competition, but paradoxically can be easier in real life confrontation. That is because not only are we likely to face a somewhat less skilled opponent, but we can also cheat to win. Punching the adversary in the face (which is outlawed in judo competition) and then executing a throw while he or she is momentarily stunned is far easier than throwing alone.

As Iain Abernethy puts it, "Blow before throw." Karate is primarily a striking art, so we must train to use punches, kicks, smashes, slaps, and other percussive movements to set up our throws for success. Even though throws are not a "go to" technique in most striking arts, they are an important tool in our repertoire so they should be practiced from time-to-time using the strength of our art to set them up as well as to finish off our opponent afterward.

CHAPTER 8

CRACK THE BACK, KILL THE ATTACK

"We must pay greater attention to keeping our bodies and minds healthy and able to heal. Yet we are making it difficult for our defenses to work."

David Suzuki

Break a Leg?

IN THE QUOTE ABOVE, DAVID SUZUKI, A Canadian professor of genetics (retired from the University of British Columbia) is talking about balance in life, in our bodies. That's a laudable goal for everyday existence, one we should all follow, yet in a fight we strive to do the opposite to our adversary. We strive to keep our opponent's body out of balance so that he or she will find it impossible to attack and difficult for their defenses to work effectively.

The human body can be broken down into several component parts. When it comes to a fight, the head and torso are key. The torso is made up of the abdomen and the thorax, or the belly and chest, which is what we will focus on here. Clearly the head, arms, and the legs are not part of the torso. It is useful to note that while the head is vital, if we remove an arm from the fight, say entangling, dislocating, or breaking it, our attacker still has another arm and two legs that can be used against us.

Don't think for a moment that breaking an arm or leg will stop a determined adversary. Experienced soldiers, law enforcement officers, and security personnel know first-hand that when adrenaline courses through a person's system during a fight they can be stabbed, shot, or badly mangled and still persevere, at least until the pain kicks in afterward. That's why we need to disrupt vital functions to stop a determined adversary.

All Right, We'll Call it a Draw

FOR READERS WHO ARE MONTY PYTHON FANS, you'll remember the Black Knight scene from their movie *Monty Python and the Holy Grail* (if unfamiliar, you can watch it on YouTube here: https://youtu.be/kRwCPUEND1U). King Arthur's dismemberment of the Black Knight is hilarious in part because it's so outrageous.

The ridiculousness of the Black Knight losing both arms and both legs yet still attempting to fight, even if only to "bite his legs off" is pretty good comedy, but it has a serious side too. Damage an adversary's limbs and, if he or she is determined enough, the fight isn't over. Nevertheless, we all realize a thrust of King Arthur's sword through the Black Knight's belly would have ended him and the fight simultaneously.

The Trunk is Key

THE HUMAN TORSO IS ALSO CALLED THE TRUNK. Trunk is a wonderful example that we are going to use here. The idea is that a tree without a trunk is a nothing more than a pile of firewood. There's no connective material to hold everything together. Similarly, a human being without their trunk is a pile of meat.

Our body is designed to protect our trunk, because the trunk contains so many vital organs that are necessary for life. And, the trunk includes one of the critical aspects of success or failure in combat—the lower lumbar region of the spine. You see, the closer we can get to the lumbar vertebrae, the more effective our attack is going to be and the weaker our adversary's defense.

In other words, if we can crack their back, we can kill the opponent's attack. This doesn't necessarily require damage to the spine; it can merely be twisting or turning things such that our adversary cannot use effective body alignment for his or her techniques. With poor balance and/or skewed alignment, defensive and offensive techniques become ineffectual.

Out of Position

ATHLETES IN MOST ANY SPORTING EVENT TEND to bend forward at their waist to achieve forward-leaning momentum. The sprinter, the football player, the baseball player, the soccer player, and the basketball player, they all seek this forward position. It allows them to move swiftly and precisely, whether their aim is to go forward, backward, or to either side. We observe this same phenomenon in Olympic judo, taekwondo, and other combat sports. And, we see it on the street too. Everyone seeks this forward-leaning platform because it is effective for athletic endeavors.

Conversely, the worst position an athlete can be in is leaning backward. Imagine a sprinter getting into the blocks to prepare for his or her run. Before the starting gun fires, they proceed to bend their upper body backward as far as they can. That would be nuts, right? Leaning backward this way, it will be impossible for them to be competitive because while everyone else has already started running they would need to re-straighten their spine and then shift forward to even begin. Leaning back while twisting to the side would be even worse.

A backward bend of the spine, whether twisted sideways or not, is a terrible platform from which to perform any athletic act. In a fight, however, this is precisely what we want, not for ourselves of course, but for the other guy. You see, if our adversary is competing against us from this un-advantageous position, it will be very difficult for him or her to remain in the game let alone to compete effectively. Consequently, our goal in a combative situation is to put an attacker into this ridiculously uncompetitive posture and thereby diminish their chance to win.

Way Out of Position

THE REASON THE LUMBAR SPINE IS SO IMPORTANT is that we use less effort to rebalance ourselves the higher up the body that an imbalance occurs. In other words, an adjustment of the head is easier than pulling our chest back into alignment, so if the lower back is bent, kinked, or twisted that will be the hardest thing to recover from. And, until our spine is properly aligned it is difficult if not impossible to move, strike, or defend ourselves in battle.

We might strike at the head hoping for a knockout, as may our adversary in return, yet if he or she has been knocked off balance any punches or kicks that make it past our defenses won't do any serious damage. This is precisely why we seek to crack the back to kill the attack. It helps us win. Every throw and takedown has an obvious element of metaphorically cracking our adversary's back, no one falls down on their own if their spine is stable, yet punches and kicks can do precisely the same things too.

Imagine blowing out an adversary's knee with a kick, stomping their limb onto the ground, and then punching or elbowing him/her in the head. Clearly this twists their spine into an untenable position, but we don't necessarily need anything that extreme to do the trick. The point is to disrupt, unbalance, and then take advantage to the opportunity that creates. The farther out of position we place the other guy (or gal), the better off we will be.

Happo No Kuzushi

HAPPO NO KUZUSHI (THE EIGHT DIRECTIONS OF unbalancing) is a very important concept in martial arts, one used by grappling and striking forms alike. The points of imbalance represent the cardinal and ordinal points of a compass, a seen in the illustration below. The cardinal points are north, south, east, and west, while the ordinal points are northeast, southeast, southwest, and northwest.

Kuzushi (unbalancing) is often thought of as merely pushing or pulling in one of those directions to knock an adversary off his or her balance, yet at more advanced levels it becomes far more than that. It turns into a mental technique as much as a physical one, breaking the adversary's rhythm to thwart his or her attack or more successfully initiate our own. This can be seen in everything from kiai (spirit shout) to changes in speed or tempo, fakes, or strikes that place him or her out of position.

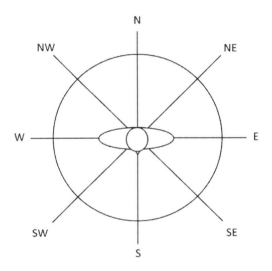

Figure 9: Happo No Kuzushi (Eight Directions of Unbalancing)

All directions of the compass hold potential for imbalance, as well as for putting an opponent onto the ground, but the two quarters of the diagram between Southwest and Southeast are the most difficult directions throw a person. The reason for this is that our eyes, hands, and feet are forward-oriented. The combination of these three elements, eyes, hands, and feet, make it easier for us to keep or regain balance when pushed from this direction. This is, in part, why hitting someone before attempting to throw them is so important.

TRAIN FOR VICTORY

EVERY MARTIAL ART, BE IT PRIMARILY SPORTING or combative, holds effective methods for unbalancing opponents. This concept is so important, and so useful, that we frequently see it taught in reality-based self-defense classes as well, seminars where participants look to master a few tactics with which they might ward off danger but are generally uninterested in pursuing long term martial arts training.

One example is the neck-crank takedown, which can be devastating when performed correctly. With the right instruction, practitioners can move from introduction to application in just a few hours.

Additional examples are legion. Find yours. Identify what your individual system does to imbalance adversaries and spend quality time working those tactics and techniques. Don't just use them on your training partners and vice versa, also practice recovering from those same imbalances so that such things will be harder to use against you in a fight. After all, as we strive to crack the back to kill our opponent's attack, so too will others attempt the same thing against us.

CHAPTER 9

PUNCHES COME IN BUNCHES

"Opportunities multiply as they are seized."

Sun Tzu

That Time Our Friend Got Swatted

AS OUR FRIEND TOLD THE STORY WE SAT FIXATED on the event. He was working with a Special Weapons and Tactics (SWAT) team in a midwestern city. SWAT is, of course, much like military special forces. They are the best operators in the agency, officers who get called into policing circumstances that have blown-up and have gone or are very close to going sideways, like hostage situations.

Our friend was playing a hostage. He was sitting on the floor in the corner of a cinderblock room. There was only one way into the room and one way out, the front door. Because blowing up or knocking down a wall could injure or kill the hostage (and ruin their training equipment), the SWAT team had no choice but to enter the room through the only door. The hostage-takers, played by their fellow police officers, knew this dynamic too. It seemed like a no-win scenario.

Suddenly there as a blast of light and noise as something exploded into the room. Our friend related that as soon as he regained his eyesight, he found himself staring up at the business end of an assault rifle. A quick pan of the room and he realized that everyone else, hostage or hostage-taker, was on the ground with a matching rife pointed at them too.

Speed, Surprise, and Violent Action

WHILE THIS WAS JUST A TRAINING SCENARIO, the flash-bang (stun) grenades were real, as was their impact on the participants. Disorientation, including temporary blindness for 5 to 10 seconds, dizziness for several minutes, and diminished hearing/ringing in the ears that lasts for hours made it challenging to think let alone move or fight. This episode, while by no means a fistfight, was an excellent example of the three most important elements of a violent encounter: (1) surprise, (2) speed, and (3) violence of action. By the time the hostage-takers could perceive the threat, let alone respond, it was too late. The SWAT team had already won.

These same factors apply to unarmed combat too. Consider the classic barroom brawl: some perceived insult turns into a verbal challenge, which escalates into a shove, and then suddenly fists start flying. Or, perhaps the aggrieved party waits out in the parking lot and sets a trap. Sucker punch or ambush, either way, there will be surprise, speed, and violence of action because in real-life fighting, punches come in bunches. Rage, strategic intent, it really doesn't matter, the dynamic remains the same. Punches come in bunches... thrown with surprise, speed, and violence of action.

Figure 10: Punches Come in Bunches

Chunking is Only for the Training Hall

AN ICONIC COMPONENT OF KARATE TRAINING is drills where we stand in place and repeatedly throw one punch or perform one block while the instructor counts aloud each repetition. The image is so symbolic that Bruce Lee included this shot in his classic movie Enter the Dragon. In tandem drills we do much the same thing. Take san dan gi (three level sequence) for example, where each partner trades off a block or punch, the other takes his or her turn, and then the sequence repeats.

This practice method is called "chunking." It is pretty much the same thing a computer does to break up long strings of information into chunks or units that it can process. Chunking is similarly used by our human brains to break complicated things into digestible chunks that are easier to commit to memory. This works good for memorization, performance by rote, but not so great for practical application.

In other words, this one and done sort of training is fine for learning fundamentals, but piss poor for application. On the street we would never throw one blow, pause to examine its effect or wait for the adversary to make a counterstrike, and then continue. The experienced violent actor knows that his or her movements must be fast, smooth, and relentless.

Fast is another word for surprise. Even if we see it coming, we may not be able to act in time to do anything about it. Smooth is fast, and relentless means when we get the advantage. Once we have it, we never give it up until the fight is over and we are safe. So, while the iconic "thousand punches in the air" is nice, we must move past chunking to the use our strikes with surprise, speed, and violence of action for success on the street.

Gain the Advantage and Never Give it Up

THIS PRINCIPLE OF SURPRISE, SPEED, AND violent action is why the SWAT teams' tactics work. Bad guys use this very same notion too; they seek to gain an advantage and never give it up until the fight is over. Even unskilled adversaries will instinctively throw a flurry of strikes in a fight. Continuous, relentless attack is a pillar of violence in action. That is what we can expect to face in a fight, and simultaneously what me must bring to the battle.

The means and methods of implementation will vary with the tactical environment. A late-night confrontation at a mini-mart differs from a barroom brawl or a fight in a hospital emergency room. The number of combatants, location, lighting, footing, obstacles in play; a variety of factors will dictate exactly how any given fight will go down, but applying the principle of punches coming in bunches helps us both prepare and prevail. Our goal is to gain advantage and never give it up until the danger is over.

TRAIN FOR VICTORY

THE KEY TO TRAINING FOR SURPRISE, SPEED, AND violent action is with dynamic drills such as *kumite* (free style sparring), where we continuously move and attack/defend while working with one or more opponents. It's vital to assure that we do not lose focus on fundamentals such as proper form and power generation while performing these techniques. All too often, especially when folks get tired, technique goes out the window and we unintentionally reinforce bad behaviors, so videorecording and debriefing these sessions is valuable.

Some systems, such as *kyokushin* karate with their 25-man *kumite*, already have this concept baked in so practitioners can leverage what comes with the program. Nevertheless, it is valuable to practice dynamic movements and relentless attack using a body opponent bag (BOB), heavy bag, or *makiwara* (striking post) from time to time too. This helps us instinctively unleash a fury of punches, kicks, and other strikes with ferocity and power when called upon to do so.

CHAPTER 10

EVERYTHING BAD FOR YOU

"We're not just going to shoot the bastards.
We're going to cut out their living guts and
use them to grease the treads of our tanks."

General George S. Patton

Everything Bad

PHYSICAL CONFLICTS ARE NASTY AFFAIRS. WE have stated many times the importance of avoiding a fight whenever possible. To escape, to not be there when things pop off, that's a laudable and often achievable goal. We've written extensively in other books about how to use awareness, avoidance, and de-escalation among other strategies to extricate oneself from nasty situations. And, we've gone on the record as being opposed to needless physical conflict.

But that doesn't mean that violence does not happen, that it won't happen to you. That doesn't mean that that it's always possible to avoid an altercation. And, there are a lot of folks out there who hold a different view about fighting… some relish the opportunity to dish out pain on others.

Don't Mess with Haku

BORN ON THE SOUTH PACIFIC ISLAND OF TONGA, 'Uli'uli Fifita is better known by his professional wrestling moniker "Haku." Haku was a top earner at one time for several World Wrestling Entertainment (WWE) productions such as the World Wrestling Federation (WWF), New Japan Pro-Wrestling (NJPW), and World Championship Wrestling (WCW). He was also acknowledged as one of the toughest men to ever battle in or out of the ring.

A legend had grown around a bar fight involving Haku. It's said that during a night of drinking the barroom became chippy, with several patrons calling out Haku and other wrestlers in the establishment as fakes. As fans we all accept that professional wrestling is scripted, yet most realize that the physicality and the violence, both contrived and sometimes real, takes a toll on the participants. In other words, the wrestling business is a business in which tough people can make a tough living.

The men heckling these wrestlers must have thought they were tough too, they were taunting a 6-foot, 2-inch tall, 275-pound professional wrestler after all, but in truth they had no idea what they were messing with. You see, when one of the hecklers pushed too far, he set Haku off. By his own admission, Haku answered the challenge of being a fake by saying, "I'll show you." Then, he reached out, grabbed the man's face, and bit his nose off! The moment went from zero to sixty instantaneously. And, the fight was on…

Imagine the shock of witnessing another person's nose being bitten off, let alone being the target of such an attack. The blood streaming from the victim's face was a clear demonstration that everything bad was in play, and Haku and fellow professional wrestler Papali'itele Max Amata Taogaga (known in the ring as Siva Afi), a 5-foot, 10-inch, 240-pound Samoan, used that shock-and-awe to clear the room.

Breakdown of a Barroom Brawl

NOTE THAT HAKU USED SURPRISE, SPEED, AND violent action to turn the tables on his heckler and did so in the extreme. His choice was next-level violence, mentally and physically going far beyond anyone's expectations of a "normal" bar brawl, to the extent that there is such a thing as a normal bar brawl. Haku was a guy used to fighting. After all, scripted though it may have been, violence was his job.

Even drunk, Haku had a plan. His very first movement was strategic and it set up everything that followed. You see, taking ahold of another person's face is only done in one of two situations, intimacy or dominance. The other guy's instinctive recoil from that first touch made the next movement, biting his nose off, easier. From that point on, he had no chance.

The tactics of fighting vary, but the opportunity to take advantage and keep that advantage is our principle here. It is the essence of "everything bad for you," which we can short-hand as EB-FYOU. This is when blocks disappear as they morph into strikes, punches come in bunches, and domination becomes inevitable. In other words, when violence is necessary and unavoidable, our goal is to get so far ahead of the count that the other guy (or gal) has no chance like that nose-less wonder who messed with the wrong Tongan.

Here's the deal, striking first leaves an opening. That opening may be small, wonderfully large, or vaporize quickly, but in the moment of the initial strike it exists. Think of how many confrontations you have seen on video or in real life with the pulling back of a fist in anger was an opening. More often than not this telegraphs the threat's first move, so those of us used to training for *sen no sen* can use it as a gift. How did that play out in the examples you've seen? Was that gift exploited or did the target get behind the count, become a victim, and lose the fight?

The opening moments of a confrontation can be a present or a penance. It's all in how we meet it. As you now know, what we do at the start sets the stage for everything that follows.

Tournament Competitor verses Street Fighter

JUMPING INTO AND BACK OUT OF RANGE IS THE core of tournament fighting strategy. Competitors understand it is an advanced, somewhat painful game of tag, with its own set of rules and referees, and strategies to fit. That doesn't mean that tournament fights are not real, but rather that they are artificial. When our opponent cannot pull our hair, gouge our eyes out, break our fingers, stomp us to the curb, or utilize any number of outlawed techniques designed to prevent serious injury and keep things moving during competition, the dynamic between what happens in the ring and outside the ring is changed.

Consequently, what wins in a tournament often stands little chance of doing so during in a serious violent encounter. Heavyweight boxer Mike Tyson may have bitten a chunk out of Evander Holyfield's ear during a match, but he was subsequently disqualified. Not only is biting illegal, we're not aware of anyone having their nose bitten off in the ring. On the street, however, it's a different story. The real world has a different set of rules and strategies than the tournament ring and we must accommodate those differences.

The good news here is that whatever system of karate (or most any martial art for that matter) that we choose to practice, it will have means and methods of using continuous attack that will make it effective on the street. That suggests that we don't need to recreate the proverbial wheel, it's already been invented for us. We need only apply the axiom EB-FYOU, leveraging the strategy and applications from our chosen system.

In other words, whenever we have to fight, we must constantly seek and exploit opportunities for dominance as they become available. This is how we prevail.

TRAIN FOR VICTORY

ONE PATH TO DISCOVERING HOW TO DOMINATE a fight is to choose a piece of our *kata* (or application set for those who practice a style that does not use *kata*) and work it as a staircase drill with a partner, applying a simple policy of striking with our closest available weapon throughout the exercise. In other words, if our right hand is closest to the opponent, that's what we hit with. If it's our left knee, we'll strike with that instead. In this fashion we increase the speed and efficiency of our applications.

Staircasing is inevitable and natural. It emulates what happens in a real-life physical confrontation. The principal of staircasing allows us to seek EB-FYOU without the hazards of presumptive entanglement. In part, that's because we only seek "perfection" in the opening moment of our encounter and then use whatever works from that point forward. Watch a few altercations on YouTube and you'll see this dynamic in action.

The staircasing drill looks like this:

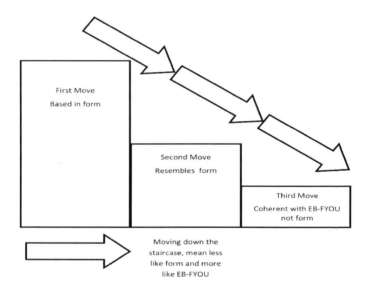

Figure 11: Staircasing Toward Everything Bad for You (EB-FYOU)

Here's how the drill is performed: Set up a pre-determined attack (say head punch by way of example) to respond to. This is discussed with our training partner ahead of time so that both parties know what will happen and can conduct the drill with as much speed and power as we are safely able.

1. For our first move, we use something from one of our *kata* (forms) to answer this opening attack. Done right it shouldn't be purely defensive as we utilize *sen no sen* to recover the initiative.
2. The second move may well be in sequence, or at least resemble the next movement in whatever form that we are using, but it is less prescribed. Simply strike with the nearest available weapon, hand, foot, elbow, knee, forehead, etc...
3. The third move leaves the gravity of the form. We take advantage of whatever opportunity presents itself with the knowledge that it likely will not be coherent with what's normally seen in *kata*. It will, however will be consistent with the principle of EB-FYOU.

This exercise will likely be messy and somewhat awkward as we begin, but focusing on target availability and the principle of everything being bad for you begins to increase. As we practice moving down the EB-FYOU staircase we should pull together all the principles discussed earlier in this book too.

This drill trains us to open up the proverbial can of whoop-ass and splatter it all over the other guy (or gal). Note that everything we do originates in our karate system of choice, so we are reinforcing mindset more than technique. In this fashion we make a giant leap toward being able to turn the tables on our assailant and defend ourselves in a real fight.

CONCLUSION

"Knowing is not enough, we must apply.
Willing is not enough, we must do."

Bruce Lee

THROUGHOUT THIS BOOK WE HAVE EXAMINED ten principles that improve the viability and efficacy of karate when it is applied in real-life, self-defense situations. These principles do not change our art form, but rather the lens through which we must view and practice it. To recap:

1. Win Before You Go In
2. Presumptive Entanglement
3. Crash the System
4. Pin to Win
5. Jabs over Grabs
6. Him Down Now
7. Throws Thrash, Takedowns Compound
8. Crack the Back, Kill the Attack
9. Punches Come in Bunches
10. Everything Bad for You

Now it is up to you. These principles are style agnostic, all about ending fights quickly. They cut to the heart of how we best apply our karate skills and training in the real world. Work with these principles, make them your own.

Practice them repeatedly. And, teach them to your fellow practitioners, for in teaching you will discover deeper understanding and internalization. In doing this you set yourself upon the immutable path to swiftness, clarity, and victory.

"DO NOT SEEK TO FOLLOW
IN THE FOOTSTEPS OF
THE WISE. SEEK WHAT
THEY SOUGHT."

✲ MATSUO BASHO ✲

THANK YOU!

THANK YOU FOR YOUR PURCHASE! PUBLISHING is an arduous process and it's folks like you who make our efforts worthwhile. With roughly 4 million new titles created every year, unbiased customer reviews are indispensable in helping readers identify books that are worth buying. To that end, if you found value from this work please let other people know. Publish an Amazon review and send us the link at http://www.stickmanpublications.com/contact/ along with your contact information and you will be entered into a drawing to win autographed versions of our four bestselling titles.

GLOSSARY

ROMANIZATION NOTE: WE HAVE PRIMARILY used the *hebon-shiki* (Hepburn) method of translating Japanese writing into the English alphabet and determining how best to spell the words (though accent marks have been excluded), as it is generally considered the most useful insofar as pronunciation is concerned. We have italicized foreign terms such that they can be readily differentiated from their English counterparts (e.g., *dan* meaning black belt rank versus *Dan*, the male familiar name for Daniel). As the Japanese (and Chinese) languages do not use capitalization, we have only capitalized those words that would be used as proper nouns in English.

Japanese is a challenging language for many English speakers to pronounce correctly. A few hints—for the most part, short vowels sound just like their English counterparts (e.g., **a** as in father, **e** as in pen). Long vowels are essentially double-length (e.g., **o** as in oil, in the word *oyo*). The **u** is nearly silent, except where it is an initial syllable (e.g., *uke*). Vowel combination **e** + **i** sounds like day (e.g., *bugeisha*), **a** + **i** sounds like alive (e.g., *bunkai*), **o** + **u** sounds like float (e.g., *tou*), and **a** + **e** sounds like lie (*kamae*). The consonant **r** is pronounced with the tip of the tongue, midway between **l** and **r** (e.g., *daruma*). Consonant combination **ts** is pronounced like cats, almost a **z** (e.g., *tsuki*).

Japanese Term	English Translation
aikido	A Japanese martial art created by Morihei Ueshiba, which translates as "the way of harmonizing life energy," that emphasizes using an attacker's strength and momentum against himself
dojo	Training hall, literally "place for learning the way"
gi (or *dogi*)	Traditional uniform used for practicing martial arts
goju ryu	An Okinawan unarmed martial art developed by Chojun Miyagi, which translates as the "hard/gentle way of the infinite fist"
happo no kuzushi	The "eight directions of unbalancing"
ippon-seoi-nage	"One-arm shoulder throw," a technique common to judo, karate, and many other martial arts
judo	A Japanese martial art (and Olympic sport) developed by Jigoro Kano that features an emphasis on throwing, grappling, choking, and joint-locking techniques
judoka	Judo practitioner, may be singular or plural
jujitsu	A (primarily) Japanese martial arts system that emphasizes holds, throws, and paralyzing blows to subdue an adversary
kakidameshi	Dueling

Japanese Term	English Translation
kansetsu waza	Joint locks
karate	A (primarily) Japanese or Okinawan martial art which emphasizes empty-hand striking techniques for self-defense
karateka	Karate practitioner, may be singular or plural
kata	"Form," a pattern of movements containing a series of logical and practical offensive and defensive techniques used in solo training
katame-waza	Grappling techniques
kenpo karate	A Japanese unarmed fighting method that can be translated as "fist law," which was brought to Japan from China about 700 years ago by the Yoshida Clan
kiai	A "spirit shout," a loud yell designed to focus one's energy and unbalance an adversary
kotegaishi	Wrist lock throw commonly found in aikido, jujitsu, and karate and other martial arts
kumite	Freestyle fighting (sparring)
kuzushi	Unbalancing
kyokushin	A style of stand-up fighting that was founded in 1964 by Masutatsu Oyama

Japanese Term	English Translation
makiwara	"Striking post," a board used for practicing karate technique that is usually affixed to or planted in the ground and padded with leather, foam, or rope
newaza	Ground fighting techniques such as chokes, pins, and joint locks
osae komi waza	Hold down techniques
randori	Free-style practice such as sparring with a fellow martial arts practitioner
samurai	A member of the warrior class in feudal Japan
san dan gi	"Three level sequence," a drill that helps new practitioners learn three basic stances, blocks, and punches
sensei	Martial arts instructor, literally "one who has come before"
shito ryu	An Okinawan unarmed martial art that was founded in 1934 by Kenwa Mabuni
shorin ryu	An Okinawan unarmed martial art meaning "small forest" that was named by Choshin Chibana in 1933 (though the system itself is much older)
shotokan	A Japanese unarmed martial art developed by Gichin Funakoshi and his son Gigo (Yoshitaka) Funakoshi

Japanese Term	English Translation
tai chi	An internal Chinese martial art practiced for health benefits and meditation in addition to self-defense, with practitioners often using extremely slow and precise movements during training
uechi ryu	An Okinawan unarmed martial art created by Kanbun Uechi in 1904
wado ryu	A Japanese unarmed martial art founded by Hironori Ohtsuka in 1934
wing chun	A traditional southern Chinese kung-fu style that utilizes both striking and "sticking" (controlling) in close-range combat to defeat one's adversaries
yakuza	Members of organized crime syndicates originating in Japan (often with transnational influence)

BIBLIOGRAPHY

Books

- Ayoob, Massad. *The Truth About Self-Protection.* New York, NY: Bantam Books (Police Bookshelf), 1983.

- Christensen, Loren and Dr. Alexis Artwohl. *Deadly Force Encounters: What Cops Need To Know To Mentally And Physically Prepare For And Survive A Gunfight.* Boulder, CO: Paladin Enterprises, Inc., 1997.

- Christensen, Loren. *Far Beyond Defensive Tactics: Advanced Concepts, Techniques, Drills, and Tricks for Cops on the Street.* Boulder, CO: Paladin Enterprises, Inc., 1998.

- Christensen, Loren. *Warriors: On Living with Courage, Discipline and Honor.* Boulder, CO: Paladin Enterprises, Inc., 2004.

- DeBecker, Gavin. *The Gift of Fear: Survival Signals That Protect Us From Violence.* New York, NY: Dell Publishing, 1998.

- Dempsey, Jack and Jack Cuddy. *Championship Fighting: Explosive Punching and Aggressive Defense.* Centerline Press 1983 (original edition was printed in 1950 in NY by Prentice Hall).

- Grossman, David A. and Loren Christensen. *On Combat: The Psychology and Physiology of Deadly Conflict in War and Peace.* Belleville, IL: PPCT Research Publications, 2004.

- Grossman, David A. *On Killing: The Psychological Cost of Learning to Kill in War and Society*. New York, NY: Little, Brown, and Company, 1995.

- Kane, Lawrence A. and Kris Wilder. *The Little Black Book of Violence: What Every Young Man Needs to Know About Fighting*. Wolfeboro, NH: YMAA, 2009.

- Kane, Lawrence A., Kris Wilder, and Sun Tzu. *Sh!t Sun Tzu Said: Classic Warfare for the Modern Mind*. Burien, WA: Stickman Publications, Inc., 2020

- Kane, Lawrence A. *Surviving Armed Assaults: A Martial Artists Guide to Weapons, Street Violence, and Countervailing Force*. Boston, MA: YMAA, 2006.

- Kane, Lawrence A., and Kris Wilder. *The Way of Kata: A Comprehensive Guide for Deciphering Martial Applications*. Boston, MA: YMAA, 2005

- Lovret, Fredrick J. *The Way and the Power: Secrets of Japanese Strategy*. Boulder, CO: Paladin Enterprises, Inc., 1987

- MacYoung, Marc. *A Professional's Guide to Ending Violence Quickly*. Boulder, CO: Paladin Enterprises, Inc., 1993.

- MacYoung, Marc. *Cheap Shots, Ambushes, and Other Lessons: A Down And Dirty Book On Streetfighting and Survival*. Boulder, CO: Paladin Enterprises, Inc., 1989.

- MacYoung, Marc. *Fists, Wits, and a Wicked Right: Surviving On the Wild Side of the Street*. Boulder, CO: Paladin Enterprises, Inc., 1991.

- MacYoung, Marc. *Floor Fighting: Stompings, Maimings, and Other Things to Avoid When a Fight Goes to the Ground*. Boulder, CO: Paladin Enterprises, Inc., 1993.

- MacYoung, Marc. *Knives, Knife Fighting, And Related Hassles: How to Survive A Real Knife Fight*. Boulder, CO: Paladin Enterprises, Inc., 1990.

- MacYoung, Marc. *Pool Cues, Beer Bottles, & Baseball Bats: Animal's Guide to Improvised Weapons for Self-Defense and Survival.* Boulder, CO: Paladin Enterprises, Inc., 1990.

- MacYoung, Marc. *Street E & E: Evading, Escaping, and Other Ways to Save Your Ass When Things Get Ugly.* Boulder, CO: Paladin Enterprises, Inc., 1993.

- Miller, Rory A. *Facing Violence: Preparing for the Unexpected.* Wolfeboro, NH: YMAA Publication Center, 2011.

- Miller, Rory A. *Force Decisions: A Citizen's Guide to Understanding How Police Determine Appropriate Use of Force.* Wolfeboro, NH: YMAA Publication Center, April 2012.

- Miller, Rory A. *Meditations on Violence: A Comparison of Martial Arts Training and Real-World Violence.* Wolfeboro, NH: YMAA Publication Center, 2008.

- Miller, Rory and Lawrence A. Kane. *Scaling Force: Dynamic Decision Making Under Threat of Violence.* Wolfeboro, NH: YMAA Publication Center, 2012.

- Miller, Rory. *Conflict Communication A New Paradigm in Conscious Communication.* Washougal, WA: Wyrd Goat Press, 2014.

- Miller, Rory. *Drills: Training for Sudden Violence (A Chiron Manual).* Washougal, WA: Wyrd Goat Press, 2011.

- Quinn, Peyton. *Real Fighting: Adrenaline Stress Conditioning through Scenario-Based Training.* Boulder, CO: Paladin Enterprises, Inc., 1996.

- Siddle, Bruce K. *Sharpening the Warrior's Edge: The Psychology and Science of Training.* Millstadt, IL: PPCT Research Publications, Inc., 1995.

- Sockut, Eugene. *Secrets of Street Survival – Israeli Style: Staying Alive in a Civilian War Zone.* Boulder, CO: Paladin Enterprises, Inc., 1995.

- Suarez, Gabe. *The Combative Perspective: The*

Thinking Man's Guide to Self-Defense. Boulder, CO: Paladin Enterprises, Inc., 2003.

- Taubert, Robert K. *Rattenkrieg! The Art and Science of Close Quarters Battle Pistol.* North Reading, MA: Saber Press, July 1, 2012.

- Wilson, William Scott and Tsunetomo Yamamoto. *Hagakure: The Book of the Samurai.* Boston, MA: Shambhala Press, 2002.

Websites

- Encyclopedia Britannica (www.britannica.com)
- Force Science Institute (www.forcescience.org)
- History Net (www.historynet.com)
- Marc MacYoung (www.nononsenselfdefense.com)
- National Institute of Mental Health (www.nimh.nih.gov)
- Psychology Today (www.psychologytoday.com)
- The Bureau of Justice Statistics (www.bjs.gov)
- The Federal Bureau of Investigation (www.fbi.gov)
- The History Channel (www.history.com)
- The People History: (www.thepeoplehistory.com)
- The Quotations Page (www.quotationspage.com)
- Unified Crime Reports (www.fbi.gov/about-us/cjis/ucr/ucr)
- United States Bureau of Labor Statistics (www.bls.gov)
- Warfare History Network (www.warfarehistorynetwork.com)

ABOUT THE AUTHORS

Kris Wilder, BCC

KRIS WAS INDUCTED INTO THE US MARTIAL ARTS Hall of Fame in 2018. He runs the West Seattle Karate Academy, a frequent destination for practitioners from around the world which also serves the local community. He has earned black belt rankings in three styles, karate, judo, and taekwondo, and often travels to conduct seminars across the United States, Canada, and Europe. His book, *The Way of Sanchin Kata*, was translated into Japanese, a rare honor for a Western karate practitioner.

A Nationally Board-Certified Life Coach and prolific author, Kris has lectured at Washington State University and Susquehanna University. He spent about 15 years in the political and public affairs arena, working for campaigns from the local to national level. During this consulting career, he was periodically on staff for elected officials. His work also involved lobbying and corporate affairs. And, he was also a member of The Order of St. Francis (OSF), one of many active Apostolic Christian Orders.

Kris is the bestselling author of 22 books, including a Beverly Hills Book Award and Presidential Prize winner, a USA Best Book Awards winner, a National Indie Excellence Awards winner, and a Next Generation Indie Book Awards winner. He has been interviewed on CNN, FOX, The Huffington Post, Thrillist, Nickelodeon, Howard Stern, and more.

Kris lives in Seattle, Washington. You can contact him directly at Kriswilder@kriswilder.com, follow him on Twitter (@kris_wilder), on Facebook (www.facebook.com/kris.wilder) or Instagram (https://www.instagram.com/thekriswilder/).

Lawrence A. Kane, COP-GOV, CSP, CSMP, CIAP

LAWRENCE WAS INDUCTED INTO THE SOURCING Industry Group (SIG) Sourcing Supernova Hall of Fame in 2018 for pioneering leadership in strategic sourcing, procurement, supplier innovation, and digital transformation. An Executive Certified Outsourcing Professional, Certified Sourcing Professional, Certified Supplier Management Professional, and Certified Intelligent Automation Professional, he currently works as a senior leader at a Fortune® 50 corporation where he gets to play with billions of dollars of other people's money and make really important decisions.

A martial artist, judicious use-of-force expert, and the bestselling author of 20 books, he has won numerous awards including the 5th Annual Beverly Hills Book Award and Presidential Prize, the 13th Annual USA Best Book Awards winner, the 11th and 14th Annual National Indie Excellence Awards winner, a Next Generation Indie Book Awards winner, 3 ForeWord Magazine Book of the Year Award finalists, 5 USA Book News Best Books Award finalists, 3 Next Generation Indie Book Awards finalists, 2 Beverly Hills Book Awards finalists, and an eLit Book Awards Bronze prize.

Since 1970, Lawrence has studied and taught traditional Asian martial arts, medieval European combat, and modern close-quarter weapon techniques. Working stadium security part-time for 26 years he was involved in hundreds of violent altercations, but got paid to watch football. A founding technical consultant to University of New Mexico's Institute of Traditional Martial Arts, he has also written hundreds of articles on martial arts, self-defense, countervailing force, and related topics.

He has been interviewed numerous times on podcasts (e.g., Art of Procurement, Negotiations Ninja Podcast), nationally syndicated and local radio shows (e.g., Biz Talk Radio, The Jim Bohannon Show), and television programs (e.g., Fox Morning News) as well as by reporters from Computerworld, Le Matin, Practical Taekwondo, Forbes, Traditional Karate, and Police Magazine, among other publications. He was once interviewed in English by a reporter from a Swiss newspaper for an article that was published in French, and found that oddly amusing.

Lawrence lives in Seattle, Washington. You can contact him directly at lakane@ix.netcom.com or connect with him on LinkedIn (www.linkedin.com/in/lawrenceakane).

AMALGAMATED WORKS BY THE AUTHORS

Non-Fiction Books

<u>Musashi's Dokkodo</u> (Kane/Wilder)

"The authors have made classic samurai wisdom accessible to the modern martial artist like never before" – **Goran Powell**, award winning author of *Chojun* and *A Sudden Dawn*

Shortly before he died, Miyamoto Musashi (1584 – 1645) wrote down his final thoughts about life for his favorite student Terao Magonojō to whom Go Rin No Sho, his famous Book of Five Rings, had also been dedicated. He called this treatise Dokkodo, which translates as "The Way of Walking Alone." This treatise contains Musashi's original 21 precepts of the Dokkodo along with five different interpretations of each passage written from the viewpoints of a monk, a warrior, a teacher, an insurance executive, and a businessman. In this fashion you are not just reading a simple translation of Musashi's writing, you are scrutinizing his final words for deeper meaning. In them are enduring lessons for how to lead a successful and meaningful life.

The Little Black Book of Violence (Kane/Wilder)

"This book will save lives!" – **Alain Burrese**, JD, former US Army 2nd Infantry Division Scout Sniper School instructor

Men commit 80% of all violent crimes and are twice as likely to become the victims of aggressive behavior. This book is primarily written for men ages 15 to 35, and contains more than mere self-defense techniques. You will learn crucial information about street survival that most martial arts instructors don't even know. Discover how to use awareness, avoidance, and de—escalation to help stave off violence, know when it's prudent to fight, and understand how to do so effectively when fighting is unavoidable.

Sh!t Sun Tzu Said (Kane/Wilder)

"If you had to choose one variant of Sun Tzu's collected work, this one should be at the top of the pile... I loved it!" – **Jeffrey-Peter Hauck**, MSc, JD, Police SGT (Ret.), LPI, CPT USA, Professor of Criminal Justice

Sun Tzu was a famous Chinese general whose mastery of strategy was so exceptional that he reportedly transformed 180 courtesans into skilled soldiers in a single training session. While that episode was likely exaggerated, historians agree that Sun Tzu defeated the Ch'u, Qi, and Chin states for King Ho-Lu, forging his empire. In 510 BC, Master Tzu recorded his winning strategies in Art of War, the earliest surviving and most revered tome of its kind. With methods so powerful they can conquer an adversary's spirit, you can use Master Tzu's strategies to overcome any challenge, from warfare to self-defense to business negotiations. This book starts with the classic 1910 translation of Art of War, adds modern and historical insight, and demonstrates how to put the master's timeless wisdom to use in your everyday life. In this fashion, the Art of War becomes accessible for the modern mind, simultaneously entertaining, enlightening, and practical.

The Big Bloody Book of Violence (Kane/Wilder)

"Implementing even a fraction of this book's suggestions will substantially increase your overall safety." – **Gila Hayes**, Armed Citizens' Legal Defense Network

All throughout history ordinary people have been at risk of violence in one way or another. Abdicating personal responsibility by outsourcing your safety to others might be the easy way out, but it does little to safeguard your welfare. In this book you'll discover what dangers you face and learn proven strategies to thwart them. Self-defense is far more than fighting skills; it's a lifestyle choice, a more enlightened way of looking at and moving through the world. Learn to make sense of "senseless" violence, overcome talisman thinking, escape riots, avert terrorism, circumvent gangs, defend against home invasions, safely interact with law enforcement, and conquer seemingly impossible odds.

Dude, The World's Gonna Punch You in the Face (Wilder/Kane)

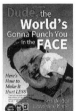

"As an emergency room physician, I see a lot of injuries. This book can save you a lot of pain and trauma, not just physical but also emotional and financial as well. Do yourself a favor, read it, and stay out of my Emergency Room." – **Jeff Cooper**, MD

We only get one shot at life. And, it's really easy to screw that up because the world wants to punch us all in the face. Hard! But, what if you knew when to duck? What if you were warned about the dangers—and possibilities— ahead of time? Here is how to man-up and take on whatever the world throws at you. This powerful book arms young men with knowledge about love, wealth, education, faith, government, leadership, work, relationships, life, and violence. It won't prevent all mistakes, nothing will, but it can keep you from making the impactful ones that you'll regret the most. This book is quick knowledge, easy to read, and brutally frank, just the way the world gives it to you, except without the pain. Read on. Learn how to see the bad things coming and avoid them.

Sensei Mentor Teacher Coach (Wilder/Kane)

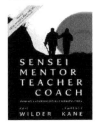

"Finally, a book that will actually move the needle in closing the leadership skills gap found in all aspects of our society." – **Dan Roberts**, CEO and President, Ouellette & Associates

Many books weave platitudes, promising the keys to success in leadership, secrets that will transform you into the great leader, the one. The fact of the matter is, however, that true leadership really isn't about you. It's about giving back, offering your best to others so that they can find the best in themselves. The methodologies in this book help you become the leader you were meant to be by bringing your goals and other peoples' needs together to create a powerful, combined vision. Learn how to access the deeper aspects of who you are, your unique qualities, and push them forward in actionable ways. Acquire this vital information and advance your leadership journey today.

Dirty Ground (Kane/Wilder)

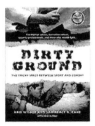

"Fills a void in martial arts training." – **Loren W. Christensen**, Martial Arts Masters Hall of Fame member

This book addresses a significant gap in most martial arts training, the tricky space that lies between sport and combat applications where you need to control a person without injuring him (or her). Techniques in this region are called "drunkle," named after the drunken uncle disrupting a family gathering. Understanding how to deal with combat, sport, and drunkle situations is vital because appropriate use of force is codified in law and actions that do not accommodate these regulations can have severe repercussions. Martial arts techniques must be adapted to best fit the situation you find yourself in. This book shows you how.

Scaling Force (Kane/Miller)

"If you're serious about learning how the application of physical force works—before, during and after the fact—I cannot recommend this book highly enough." - **Lt. Jon Lupo**, New York State Police

Conflict and violence cover a broad range of behaviors, from intimidation to murder, and require an equally broad range of responses. A kind word will not resolve all situations, nor will wristlocks, punches, or even a gun. This book introduces the full range of options, from skillfully doing nothing to employing deadly force. You will understand the limits of each type of force, when specific levels may be appropriate, the circumstances under which you may have to apply them, and the potential costs, legally and personally, of your decision. If you do not know how to succeed at all six levels covered in this book there are situations in which you will have no appropriate options. More often than not, that will end badly.

Surviving Armed Assaults (Kane)

"This book will be an invaluable resource for anyone walking the warrior's path, and anyone who is interested in this vital topic." - **Lt. Col. Dave Grossman**, Director, Warrior Science Group

A sad fact is that weapon-wielding thugs victimize 1,773,000 citizens every year in the United States alone. Even martial artists are not immune from this deadly threat. Consequently, self-defense training that does not consider the very real possibility of an armed attack is dangerously incomplete. You should be both mentally and physically prepared to deal with an unprovoked armed assault at any time. Preparation must be comprehensive enough to account for the plethora of pointy objects, blunt instruments, explosive devices, and deadly projectiles that someday could be used against you. This extensive book teaches proven survival skills that can keep you safe.

The 87—Fold Path to Being the Best Martial Artist (Kane/ Wilder)

"The 87—Fold Path contains unexpected, concise blows to the head and heart... you don't have a chance, but to examine and retool your way of life." – **George Rohrer**, Executive and Purpose Coach, MBA, CPCC, PCC

Despite the fact that raw materials in feudal Japan were mediocre at best, bladesmiths used innovative techniques to forge some of the finest swords imaginable for their samurai overlords. The process of heating and folding the metal removed impurities, while shaping and strengthening the blades to perfection. The end result was strong yet supple, beautiful and deadly. As martial artists we utilize a similar process, forging our bodies through hard work, perseverance, and repetition. Knowing how to fight is important, clearly, yet if you do not find something larger than base violence attached your efforts it becomes unsustainable. *The 87-Fold Path* provides ideas for taking your training beyond the physical that are uniquely tailored for the elite martial artist.

How to Win a Fight (Kane/Wilder)

"It is the ultimate course in self-defense and will help you survive and get through just about any violent situation or attack." – **Jeff Rivera**, bestselling author

More than 3,000,000 Americans are involved in a violent physical encounter every year. Develop the fortitude to walk away when you can and prevail when you must. Defense begins by scanning your environment, recognizing hazards and escape routes, and using verbal de-escalation to defuse tense situations. If a fight is unavoidable, the authors offer clear guidance for being the victor, along with advice on legal implications, including how to handle a police interview after the altercation.

Lessons from the Dojo Floor (Wilder)

"Helps each reader, from white belt to black belt, look at and understand why he or she trains." – **Michael E. Odell**, *Isshin-Ryu* Northwest Okinawa Karate Association

In the vein of Dave Lowry, a thought-provoking collection of short vignettes that entertains while it educates. Packed with straightforward, easy, and quick to read sections that range from profound to insightful to just plain amusing, anyone with an affinity for martial arts can benefit from this material. This book educates, entertains, and ultimately challenges every martial artist from beginner to black belt.

<u>Martial Arts Instruction</u> (Kane)

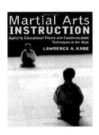

"Boeing trains hundreds of security officers, Kane's ideas will help us be more effective." – **Gregory A. Gwash**, Chief Security Officer, The Boeing Company

While the old adage, "those who can't do, teach," is not entirely true, all too often "those who can do" cannot teach effectively. This book is unique in that it offers a holistic approach to teaching martial arts; incorporating elements of educational theory and communication techniques typically overlooked in *budo* (warrior arts). Teachers will improve their abilities to motivate, educate, and retain students, while students interested in the martial arts will develop a better understanding of what instructional method best suits their needs.

<u>The Way of Kata</u> (Kane/Wilder)

"This superb book is essential reading for all those who wish to understand the highly effective techniques, concepts, and strategies that the kata were created to record." – **Iain Abernethy**, British Combat Association Hall of Fame member

The ancient masters developed *kata*, or "formal exercises," as fault—tolerant methods to preserve their unique, combat-proven fighting systems. Unfortunately, they also deployed a two-track system of instruction where only the select inner circle that had gained a master's trust and respect would be taught the powerful hidden applications of *kata*. The theory of deciphering *kata* was once a great mystery revealed only to trusted disciples of the ancient masters in order to protect the secrets of their systems. Even today, while the basic movements of *kata* are widely known, the principles and rules for understanding *kata* applications are largely unknown. This groundbreaking book unveils these methods, not only teaching you how to analyze your *kata* to understand what it is trying to tell you, but also helping you to utilize your fighting techniques more effectively.

The Way of Martial Arts for Kids (Wilder)

"Written in a personable, engaging style that will appeal to kids and adults alike." – **Laura Weller**, Guitarist, The Green Pajamas

Based on centuries of traditions, martial arts training can be a positive experience for kids. The book helps you and yours get the most out of every class. It shows how just about any child can become one of those few exemplary learners who excel in the training hall as well as in life. Written to children, it is also for parents as well. After all, while the martial arts instructor knows his art, no one knows his/her child better than the parent. Together you can help your child achieve just about anything... The advice provided is straightforward, easy to understand, and written with a child-reader in mind so that it can either be studied by the child and/or read together with the parent to assure solid results.

The Way of Sanchin Kata (Wilder)

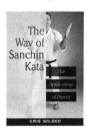

"This book has been sorely needed for generations!" – **Philip Starr**, National Chairman, Yiliquan Martial Arts Association

When karate was first developed in Okinawa it was about using technique and extraordinary power to end a fight instantly. These old ways of generating remarkable power are still accessible, but they are purposefully hidden in *sanchin kata* for the truly dedicated to find. This book takes the practitioner to new depths of practice by breaking down the form piece-by-piece, body part by body part, so that the very foundation of the *kata* is revealed. Every chapter, concept, and application is accompanied by a "Test It" section, designed for you to explore and verify the *kata* for yourself. *Sanchin kata* really comes alive when you feel the thrill of having those hidden teachings speak to you across the ages through your body. Simply put, once you read this book and test what you have learned, your karate will never be the same.

Journey: The Martial Artist's Notebook (Kane/Wilder)

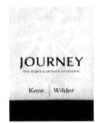

"Students who take notes progress faster and enjoy a deeper understanding than those who don't. Period." – **Loren W. Christensen**, Martial Arts Masters Hall of Fame inductee

As martial arts students progress through the lower ranks it is extraordinarily useful for them to keep a record of what they have learned. The mere process of writing things down facilitates deeper understanding. This concept is so successful, in fact, that many schools require advanced students to complete a thesis or research project concurrent with testing for black belt rank, advancing the knowledge base of the organization while simultaneously clarifying and adding depth to each practitioner's understanding of his or her art. Just as Bruce Lee's notes and essays became *Tao of Jeet Kune Do*, perhaps someday your training journal will be published for the masses, but first and foremost this notebook is by you, for you. This is where the deeper journey on your martial path toward mastery begins.

The Way to Black Belt (Kane/Wilder)

"It is so good I wish I had written it myself." – **Hanshi Patrick McCarthy**, Director, International *Ryukyu* Karate Research Society

Cut to the very core of what it means to be successful in the martial arts. Earning a black belt can be the most rewarding experience of a lifetime, but getting there takes considerable planning. Whether your interests are in the classical styles of Asia or in today's Mixed Martial Arts (MMA), this book prepares you to meet every challenge. Whatever your age, whatever your gender, you will benefit from the wisdom of master martial artists around the globe, including Iain Abernethy, Dan Anderson, Loren Christensen, Jeff Cooper, Wim Demeere, Aaron Fields, Rory Miller, Martina Sprague, Phillip Starr, and many more, who share more than 300 years of combined training experience. Benefit from their guidance during your development into a first-class black belt.

Wolves in Street Clothing (Wilder/ Hollingsworth)

"Teaches folks to rekindle tools that are already in us—already in our DNA—and have been there for thousands of years." – **Ron Jarvis**, Tracker, Outdoorsman, Self-Defense Instructor

This book gives you a new light in which to see human predatory behavior. As we move farther and farther from our roots insulating ourselves in technology and air-conditioned homes we get disconnected from the inherent and innate aspects of understanding the precursors to violent behavior. Violence is not always emotionally bound, often and in the animal kingdom is simply a tool to access a needed resource—or to protect an essential resource. Distance, encroachment, and signals are keys to avoiding a predator. Why would a cougar attack a man after a bike ride? Why would a bear attack a man in a hot tub? Why would a thug rob one person and not another? The predatory animal mind holds many of the keys to the answer to these questions. Learn drills that will help you tune your focus and move through life safer and more aware of your surroundings.

<u>70-Second Sensei</u> (Kane/Wilder)

"I'll let you in on a secret. The 70-Second Sensei is a gateway drug. It's short, easy to read, and useful. It has stuff in it that will make you a better instructor. Even a better person." — **Rory Miller**, Chiron Training

Once you have mastered the physical aspects of your martial art, it is time to take it to the next level—to lead, to teach, to leave a legacy. This innovative book shows you how. Sensei is a Japanese word, commonly translated as "teacher," which literally means "one who has come before." This term is usually applied to martial arts instructors, yet it can signify anyone who has blazed a trail for others to follow. It applies to all those who have acquired valuable knowledge, skills, and experience and are willing to share their expertise with others while continuing to grow themselves. After all, setting an example that others wish to emulate is the very essence of leadership. Clearly you cannot magically become an exemplary martial arts instructor in a mere 70-seconds any more than a businessperson can transform his or her leadership style from spending 60-seconds perusing The One Minute Manager. You can, however, devote a few minutes a day to honing your craft. It is about giving back, offering your best to others so that they can find the best in themselves. And, with appreciation, they can pay it forward...

<u>The Contract Professional's Playbook</u> (Nyden/Kane)

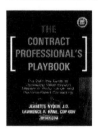

"While early career practitioners may understand the value of drafting, negotiating, and managing exceptional contracts, they often struggle to master the requisite skills. This comprehensive manual helps structure the negotiation process, thereby minimizing the perilous process of trial-and-error, expediting competency with leading practices and tools that can help reduce risk and speed outcomes for both buy-side and sell-side alike." — **Gregg Kirchhoefer**, P.C., IAOP Leadership Hall of Fame Member

Ever increasing demand for performance- and outcome-based agreements stems from pressure for enterprises to drive greater value from their strategic customer/supplier relationships. To achieve expected performance, contractual relationships are increasingly complex and interdependent, requiring more stakeholders be involved in the decision making. Unfortunately for contract professionals held accountable to these requirements there has been little in the way of resources that answer their "how to" questions about drafting, negotiating, and managing performance- and outcome-based agreements. Until now! *The Contract Professional's Playbook* (and corresponding eLearning program) walks subject matter experts who may be new to complex contracting step-by-step through all aspects of the contract life cycle. Invaluable competencies include identifying and managing risk, increasing influence with stakeholders, developing pricing models, negotiating complex deals, and governing customer-supplier relationships to avoid value leakage in the midst of constant change. It's an invaluable resource that raises the bar for buy-side and sell-side practitioners alike.

There are Angels in My Head! (Wilder)

"This is not a book on doctrine, dogma or collection of creeds to memorize in order to impress others with knowledge. This is a practical application of your participation in a new experience. Here you will find your questions answered even before they are asked." – **Br. Rich Atkinson**, Order of St. Francis

The unexplainable has happened. A prayer has been answered, a gift has been given, a communication has occurred... Is it the voice of God, or the voices in your head? Here's how to find out: In this groundbreaking book, you will discover the organization of the mystical experience. Based on the classic works of G. B Scaramelli, an 18th Century Jesuit Priest, Wilder brings modern relevance to any person to apply to their journey as they seek the Divine. Using examples and principles from Christianity and other religions, Wilder demonstrates that mankind's profound mystical experience crosses all cultures and religions.

Fiction Books

Blinded by the Night (Kane)

"Kane's expertise in matters of mayhem shines throughout." – **Steve Perry**, bestselling author

Richard Hayes is a Seattle cop. After 25 years on the force he thinks he knows everything there is to know about predators. Rapists, murderers, gang bangers, and child molesters are just another day at the office, yet commonplace criminals become the least of his problems when he goes hunting for a serial killer and runs into a real monster. The creature not only attacks him, but merely gets pissed off when he shoots it. In the head. Twice! Surviving that fight is only the beginning. Richard discovers that the vampire he destroyed was the ruler of an eldritch realm he never dreamed existed. By some archaic rule, having defeated the monster's sovereign in battle, Richard becomes their new king. When it comes to human predators, Richard is a seasoned veteran, yet with paranormal ones he is but a rookie. He must navigate a web of intrigue and survive long enough to discover how a regular guy can tangle with supernatural creatures and prevail.

Legends of the Masters (Kane/Wilder)

"It is a series of (very) short stories teaching life lessons. I'm going to bring it out when my nephews are over at family dinners for good discussion starters. A fun read!" – **Angela Palmore**

Storytelling is an ancient form of communication that still resonates today.

An engaging story told and retold shares a meaningful message that can be passed down through the generations. Take fables such as *The Boy Who Cried Wolf* or *The Tortoise and the Hare*, who hasn't learned a thing or two from these ancient tales? This book retools Aesop's lesser-known fables, reimagining them to meet the needs and interests of modern martial artists. Reflecting upon the wisdom of yesteryear in this new light will surely bring value for practitioners of the arts today.

DVDs

121 Killer Appz (Wilder/Kane)

"Quick and brutal, the way karate is meant to be." – **Eric Parsons**, Founder, Karate for Life Foundation

You know the *kata*, now it is time for the applications. *Gekisai (dai ni), Saifa, Seiyunchin, Seipai, Kururunfa, Suparinpei, Sanseiru, Shisochin,* and *Seisan kata* are covered. If you ever wondered what purpose a move from a *Goju Ryu* karate form was for, wonder no longer. This DVD contains no discussion, just a no-nonsense approach to one application after another. It illuminates your *kata* and stimulates deeper thought on determining your own applications from the *Goju Ryu* karate forms.

Sanchin Kata: Three Battles Karate Kata (Wilder)

"A cornucopia of martial arts knowledge." – **Shawn Kovacich**, endurance high-kicking world record holder (as certified by the Guinness Book of World Records)

A traditional training method for building karate power, *sanchin kata* is an ancient form. Some consider it the missing link between Chinese kung fu and Okinawan karate. This program breaks down the form piece by piece, body part by body part, so that the hidden details of the *kata* are revealed. This DVD complements the book <u>*The Way of Sanchin Kata*</u>, providing in-depth exploration of the form, with detailed instruction of the essential posture, linking the spine, generating power, and demonstration of the complete *kata*.

<u>Scaling Force</u> (Miller/Kane)

"Kane and Miller have been there, done that and have the t—shirt. And they're giving you their lessons learned without requiring you to pay the fee in blood they had to in order to learn them. That is priceless." – **M. Guthrie**, Federal Air Marshal

Conflict and violence cover a broad range of behaviors, from intimidation to murder, and they require an equally broad range of responses. A kind word will not resolve all situations, nor will wristlocks, punches, or even a gun. Miller and Kane explain and demonstrate the full range of options, from skillfully doing nothing to applying deadly force. You will learn to understand the limits of each type of force, when specific levels may be appropriate, the circumstances under which you may have to apply them, and the potential cost of your decision, legally and personally. If you do not know how to succeed at all six levels, there are situations in which you will have no appropriate options. That tends to end badly. This DVD complements the book <u>Scaling Force</u>.